The Vagabond's Breakfast

The Vagabond's Breakfast

Richard
Gwyn

ALCEMI

First impression: 2011

© Richard Gwyn, 2011

Published with the financial support of the Welsh Books Council

Editor: Gwen Davies
Cover design: Matthew Tyson

ISBN: 978-0-9560125-5-5

Printed on acid-free and partly-recycled paper.
Published by Alcemi and printed and bound in Wales by
Y Lolfa Cyf., Talybont, Ceredigion SY24 5HE
e-mail ylolfa@ylolfa.com
website www.alcemi.eu
tel 01970 832 304
fax 01970 832 782

For Rose, Sioned and Rhiannon Gwyn.
And for Lluís Peñaranda (1947–2010)
in memory of our friendship.

Je est un autre
(I is someone else)
Arthur Rimbaud

Now the rainman gave me two cures
Then he said, 'Jump right in'
The one was Texas medicine
The other was just railroad gin
An' like a fool I mixed them
An' it strangled up my mind
An' now people just get uglier
An' I have no sense of time
Bob Dylan

Yesterday evening, on entering my study, I saw the shadow of a stranger escaping through the window. I tried to pursue him, but I found no trace of him. Often I seem to hear people hidden in the bushes around the house, especially at night.
Italo Calvino

1

Many years ago, it was Boxing Day – that much I remember – I was walking along an empty Mediterranean beach. The dull, overcast morning complemented my hangover. My life was a mess. In spite of an education and no lack of opportunities, I had become an aimless wanderer: a vagabond, a drunk, and occasional agricultural labourer.

I paddled barefoot through the shallow water, up and down, clutching my shoes. Small waves broke and spilled onto the shore, lapped at my feet. Because I was not looking where I was going I would have walked straight into it, but the stench made me stop in my tracks. A pair of gulls shuffled away angrily and flew off.

At first I could not make it out. It was a great grey mess of something, encased by a dark rim, abuzz with bluebottles. A brown carapace enclosed the chaos within, which was squirming with maggot life, slithering shapes burrowing and feeding in the remnants of purple and yellow flesh. When I realised that it was a giant turtle my revulsion gave way to the kind of melancholy that could only be induced by the sight of a dead and stranded creature eaten up by worms and grubs and gulls on a deserted beach. There was nothing to do but stare at it.

My friend Peter died that Boxing Day. He died a drunkard's death, a beggar on the streets of Athens. It may be a coincidence, but the poet and bouzouki player, Hubert Tsarko, another close friend of Peter's and of mine, told me that on the same day he had encountered the corpse of a sheep, rotting on the roadside outside the house where he was staying in the French Pyrenees. This replication of dead animals did not surprise me: things often seem to happen this way, as though there were a bizarre reflective symmetry at work in the universe, to which we commonly remain oblivious, but which manifests itself nonetheless, a fragile and tenuous architecture, superimposed on the structures of an oblivious world.

2

Hepatic encephalopathy is caused by the effect on the brain of toxic substances which have accumulated in the blood as a result of liver failure. [It] may cause impaired consciousness, memory loss, personality changes, tremors, seizures, stupor and coma.

BMA Complete Family Health Encyclopaedia

April 2007

My liver has been invaded by a virus. Last December, I was given a year to live, unless a suitable donor is found. Even if I receive a transplant, there are significant dangers: the new liver will not cure me of the viral hepatitis from which I suffer, but will in turn become infected. However, a transplant will, in the language of lifespan economics, buy me time.

Along with the diseased liver, I have a creeping madness, gases that gather in my gut and infiltrate the brain. I call it brain fog, but the doctors use another term: *hepatic encephalopathy*. One of the ironies of the condition is that it is almost impossible to say it whilst suffering from it. I wander around the house at night, unable to sleep, speaking to people who are not here. I have a tendency to conjure accomplices from the darkness. And I forget things that are supposed to have happened, while remembering things that probably did not.

One night, I climb to the loft of the house, where my study is located, in search of a cigarette lighter. When I step into the room, swaying under the dual onslaught of sleep deprivation and brain fog, I am on a mission. I have a cheap lighter in my hand, but it will not suffice, since according to the demented logic of some fleeting obsession, the lighter I am searching for has to be white, and the one in my hand is blue, an aberration. I spot the power lead that connects my laptop to the mains, and it terminates in a rectangular white fixture, which I remove, thinking it might also function as a lighter, and I attempt to light it with the blue one, convinced that the only way to ignite a lighter is with another lighter. I can smell burning plastic, but because of the defect in my cognitive wiring am not immediately able to connect the smell with my own activity, until I realise that the melting fixture is burning my fingers. I am, at that moment, aware of myself as an alien presence, an utter anomaly, a man standing alone in his study having attempted, unsuccessfully, to set fire to a computer, or – which is the same thing – to his memory. The next day I find the blackened remains of the fixture hanging from my desk.

On another occasion, Rhiannon, my fourteen-year-old daughter, discovers me downstairs in the living-room trying to stuff a large blue alarm clock with bread. I stand there, in an agony of concentration, wedging a doughy ball into the mechanism with my thumb. I am muttering: *This happens all the time.* At least, this is what my daughter tells me: I have no memory of the event.

I search in vain for any purpose or symbolism behind these temporary losses of reason, or even of basic orientation. Besides, there is little opportunity for reflection of this kind. One evening, Rose, my wife, finds me walking in circles around the bedroom, and I will not respond to any questions from her other than by raising one arm and saying 'No' in a loud voice, flapping one arm like an acolyte of Mussolini, and going off into sudden quieter monologues, barely audible at times, and not consistently in English, but drifting off, on occasion, into other languages, both familiar and invented. Eventually I calm down, but early the next morning Rose cannot wake me from sleep, and has to call emergency services to take me to hospital. I do not recognise her or anybody else, and am in a state of semi-consciousness, which declines, alarmingly for Rose, into semi-coma. I remember nothing at all about that night or the following day. In the intensive care unit, a doctor tells Rose that I might not pull through, that it is touch and go. I later discover that only one in five patients survives a coma brought on by encephalopathy.

Before I am fully unconscious, six paramedics and male nurses try to sedate me, and I fight them off with flailing limbs. Rose intercedes, trying to calm me, mutters soothing words, since the efforts of the paramedics are not successful, but she cannot restrain me, my body is out of control and not responding to any instructions. One of the nursing staff thinks I am drunk; Rose informs her pointedly that I haven't drunk alcohol for many years.

But, despite my abstinence, viral hepatitis is destroying my liver, reducing that organ to end-state cirrhosis. As one reliable medical website puts it: "Liver cirrhosis in the advanced state is characterized by protein wasting, as indicated by the loss of muscle mass, hypoalbuminemia, and an abnormal amino acid profile. The protein wasting condition cirrhosis is associated with a poor prognosis and reduced survival." Once you've reached this stage, the chips are in.

Cirrhosis of the liver, duodenal ulcers, perforated oesophagus, thrombocytopenia, umbilical and inguinal hernias, ruptured varices: the prognosis is poor, and the failure of my liver to process proteins causes ammonia to seep to the brain, making me temporarily insane. I can write this in a moment of lucidity, fully aware that another attack is most likely imminent. I might have one now, as I sit writing at my desk, though the chances of this are reduced, apparently, by limiting my intake of protein, while consuming a lot of carbohydrates. They have also given me some medicine to help with the encephalopathy, which makes a person shit at least three times a day, often more. It accelerates the digestive and excretory process. In this way, the toxins passing through the liver have less time to transform into ammonia and cloud the brain. I avoid madness by shitting more. It amuses me, the way that the wellbeing of brain and bowels are so movingly interconnected. Get the crap out before it gets to the brain.

Like many sick people, I engage in a form of denial about the state of my health. However, this denial is facilitated by the remarkable sense of wellbeing, of catharsis even, that I enjoy on release from this last frightening episode in hospital, following my collapse.

I am in the bathroom at home the next morning when I experience what can only be described as a sort of epiphany. Starting as a trickle, my mind gradually becomes flooded with a delirious outpouring of ideas, bustling with each other for an outlet, and the clarity of my thought, in contrast to the confused and foggy torpor of preceding weeks, has the impact of a revelation. As I stand under the shower of warm water, the spring sunshine flooding through the bathroom window, I am overtaken by a physical premonition of wellbeing, of good health and energy, and I become convinced that the *power of the imagination* will guide me through the process of healing, and that the means to achieve this will be through my work, through the poems and stories I write. With that realisation comes, in rapid succession, a summary list of tasks: articles, projects, entire books, which until then have managed only the vaguest delineation, assume a bewildering clarity and, in the fashion of a sculptor who has been staring at a block of marble for an intolerable age, and who then sees, down to the finest detail, the figure that lies hidden within the stone, I know exactly what I have to do. I sort these embryonic works in my mind, and pursue each one in turn for a while – each cocooned in the potential of its eventual completion – and with a joyous certainty bubbling inside my brain, I step out of the shower, dry myself, and rush up to my study, noting down all the ideas that have occurred to me in the bathroom.

It is as if all this energy, all this creative power, has lain dormant, suppressed by inertia during the last few months, in which I have been incapable of writing anything, of even thinking coherently; and it is my *illness itself* that has plunged me deep into that dark, secret, unconscious place where, paradoxically, new ideas are born. I have surfaced from the dark and hollow pit and, with the bathroom luminous with sunlight and the water rushing over me, everything seems to slot sublimely into place.

It is much later that night, riveted to the white noise of the TV, that I reflect on what has happened, and realise there is something deeply suspect about this degree of euphoria.

3

Liver cirrhosis is known to be incurable, and even though a person might live with mild cirrhosis for many years, once a patient such as myself has entered what is comfortingly known as 'end stage' cirrhosis, there is no remedy other than liver transplantation, or death (itself a remedy of sorts). Until quite recently, the notion of being healed of cirrhosis would have been unimaginable; and even now, in order for me to survive, someone else – a stranger – has to die. In spite of the advances being made in the development of indigenous cell cultures, which should result, eventually, in people being able to grow their own replacement organs, the telephone will only ring to summon me to hospital because someone who has pledged their liver to medical science has passed away, or even more disturbingly, is about to; and that incites a very confused range of emotions.

In the cold hours before dawn, as I sit at the keyboard, disoriented and insane with sleeplessness, I rather doubt that the transplant will ever happen. I will either have to wait so long for the right organ that my body will be too weak to undergo the arduous operation, or else I will suffer another, terminal episode of encephalopathy. It is not surprising that I succumb to these doubts, but I do resist them.

And then there is the thorny issue of my moral entitlement to a transplant. Much has been written on this theme, and with the rising demand for organs, and the failure of government in getting people to make 'lifestyle choices' that stop them from wrecking their livers, such debates are likely to continue. But, unlike other hepatitis C patients with whom I have spoken, I have not suffered discrimination based on moral censure. It has been decided, following the criteria by which these judgements are made, that I am a worthy candidate for transplant. I cannot argue with that, though others may.

I have no idea when I acquired the virus that is killing me, though at times I cannot help but reflect on what ultimately caused this state of affairs, this breakdown of the body and the senses. Remarkably, my illness has nothing to do with the damage done to my liver by alcoholism. I was able to recover from that addiction many years ago, and under normal circumstances the liver, whose powers of recuperation are astounding, would have regenerated of its own accord. But I need to retrace my way through two decades of reckless living; not in order to track the precise moment when I carelessly contracted hep C – there are several candidate dates, spread over a few years of sporadic intravenous drug use in my early twenties, along with a couple of suspect blood transfusions – but in order to try and make sense of the *present*. I need to try and hold the present in place – because it is so fragile – by propping it up with what I can remember of the past. By recounting the story, or fragments of the story, perhaps I can achieve a better understanding of what this illness is telling me, even if that account is dislocated, fails to cohere, and lacks resolution. It seems to me that the course of one's life is determined by serendipitous meetings and improbable acts of entropy, rather than by expecting, or willing some coherent pattern to emerge, one by which we can plot our track like doomed explorers.

Most people who are ill wish to imagine the story of their illness as one of *restitution*, in which health is regarded as the normal condition to which they will be restored. According to the medical sociologist Arthur Frank the basic plot of their narrative goes something like this: "Yesterday I was healthy, today I'm sick, but tomorrow I'll be healthy again." The restitution narrative is the one that other people want to hear and which provides the medical care system with its *raison d'être*. Counteracting this is the *chaos* narrative, which contravenes the principles of restitution. Its plot imagines no return to wellness. Chaotic stories reflect the chaotic trajectory of the illness, lacking causality or sense. Chaos negates the expectation that in life one event leads to another: for this reason, chaos stories are unbearable. But even narratives of restitution contain within them, or are subject to diversion by, hostile or chaotic forces. Sometimes the course of an illness *does* descend into a state of chaos, and from this perspective restitution seems a distant dream. My illness experience has exposed me to both narratives, but neither of them is sufficient in itself.

Susan Sontag has written that illness is another country, a kind of parallel existence with its own laws and language: "Illness is the night-side of life, a more onerous citizenship. Everyone who is born holds

15

dual citizenship, in the kingdom of the well and in the kingdom of the sick." When we are ill we learn to speak the language of illness, and not only by describing it, by learning its terms and conditions, its secret passwords. We might think we know our disease and through our knowledge gain some degree of power over it. The way we do this is through our narratives, through the stories we tell, in which we attempt to contain and direct the course of our disease. But I have found, of late, that the disease keeps intruding on my narrative, like an over-protective author, ridiculing my attempts to corral it into a story of quest or of restitution. I find its presence in the notebooks I inscribe by hand at night, the illegible scrawl, the spider trail of ink on the page as I stumble through words as if bereft, confined to an inferior idiom, a sort of mumbling litany, a language of decrement and insanity. I have learned the vocabulary and syntax of the disease which is in my blood, but it has now spawned this new complication, the encephalopathy that seeps into the brain, causing confusion and a vague sense of regret.

4

My stay in hospital clashes with a planned family trip to Madrid, and we miss the flight. We decide to go to Spain for Easter anyhow, not to Madrid, but to Rabós, a small village in the Albera Mountains of Catalunya, where we own a ramshackle house, currently more of a project than a home. How I came to find this village merits a digression. I have nothing against digressions; after all, on a cosmic scale, every story begins as a digression from the one that came before, stretching back to the first syllable of recorded speech.

In the spring of 1988 I had returned to Catalunya after spending much of the winter in Andalucia. I had been wandering around Europe for eight years and was in a bad way, undernourished, and suffering anxiety attacks brought on by delirium tremens whenever I attempted to curb my drinking. I needed help with my addiction, but did not know how to set about getting it, and I arrived in the town of Figueres at five o'clock one morning, in a lamentable condition, having hitchhiked from the south of Spain. I was under no illusion as to the source of my problems, and yet the prospect of a life without alcohol was unthinkable. I was, at the time – providing I could get hold of it – drinking upwards of seven litres of wine a day. Although I had very little money, this dosage was usually achievable, since in the countries I preferred wine was dirt cheap. Because of my material circumstances, drink provided a kind of solace, and I was not able to think much beyond the immediate demands of the here and now. Or, perhaps this is entirely wrong; perhaps I was under no illusion that alcohol provided 'solace'. It provided me, for much of the time, with the illusion of my own omnipotence, even a bizarre sense of immortality. The novelist Marguerite Duras, who knew a thing or two about intemperate drinking, had the following to say: "Alcohol doesn't console, it doesn't fill up anyone's psychological gaps, all it replaces is the lack of God. It doesn't comfort man. On the contrary, it encourages him in his folly, it transports him to the supreme regions where he is master of his own destiny." Nowhere is this folly of being the master of one's destiny more blindingly apparent – or more problematic – than among drunks.

In Figueres, I called in on a Catalan friend, the painter Lluís Peñaranda, who offered to help me out. He made space for me in a spare room, and offered me work on a house he was restoring in the village of Espolla, not far from Figueres. While staying with Lluís, an eminently sober person, I managed to contain my drinking, at least temporarily – at times I had to take a break from the endless round of inebriation, I would become too sick and exhausted to continue – and my daily visits to Espolla, where I cleaned wooden beams, tiled and painted, cleared the patio and mixed cement for the builder, provided me with free time in which to explore the Albera mountains, which form a cordon between the high Pyrenees and the sea. One afternoon, with no particular plan in mind, I set off through the twisting orchard lanes out of Espolla, and walked to the nearby village of Rabós.

There were a few hungry-looking dogs, and many cats, the latter intent on studying me and avoiding the dogs. In the middle of the afternoon the village seemed deserted, but despite its emptiness the place retained a curious appeal, a sense of being abandoned in an earlier decade. It was an unassuming and untidy place, built into the hillside, old houses clustered randomly around a small eleventh-century church, sheep huddled on a patch of dusty ground below the square. I walked through the narrow cobbled streets, barely wide enough for a car, and vowed to myself that if ever I was able to sort my life out, this was where I would like to live.

So, nearly twenty years on, I feel that I might convalesce better in Rabós than anywhere, with the pristine air and gentle walks in the surrounding hills. But it is cold and overcast for most of the time, and I don't get out much. My older daughter, Sioned, is revising for her GCSE exams, and keeps me company as we wrap ourselves in blankets like convalescents against the chill and sip hot infusions. Although I write a little in the mornings, I quickly realise that I am not properly recovered from this latest attack. Moreover, the insomnia, from which I have suffered for several years, is relentless.

One night, despairing of sleep, I drive to the town of Verges, an hour away, where there is a famous Maundy Thursday parade which tracks the final events in the life of Jesus, culminating at around two in the morning with 'The Dance of Death' enacted by figures garbed as skeletons. I spend the first half of the parade on the terrace of a house belonging to a friend of a friend, adjacent to the church itself, while the parade assembles: figures dressed as Roman centurions, villains and victims in the paschal story; candle bearers, a beating drum. The parade leaves the church square at around midnight and trails through the town, due to return to the church two or three hours later for the Dance of Death.

The skeleton people move with a strange, ponderous, hopping motion, looking around as they do so; their impassive masked gaze tells me no one is exempt from the gaze of Death. The last dancer (a child? a midget?) twists in the air as he leaps. He seems to be suspended for an impossibly long time several feet above the ground before landing again, although I know this is not possible. I know it is an illusion created by his bizarre attire, by his personification of death itself – free from the normal constraints of gravity – and by the dislocation from everyday expectations that a carnival or fiesta affords. He carries a scythe, which he waves casually about him as he moves, slicing down imaginary victims. I stand on the terrace and consider the implications. There is something strictly camp about this masque of death, this graveyard humour, as though the participants were self-consciously responding to the requirement to carry out an entertainment or diversion. Yet, simultaneously, their performance conveys its core message, that no matter how one lives one's life, this is how things will end, with all the paraphernalia of Death's theatre; the dancing mutant, the grinning skull, the waving of a scythe, the half-pirouette with eyes scanning the audience. No birds flutter and tweet around Death as they did with Saint Francis of Assisi. The birds have taken flight on his approach and the plane tree he passes is silent and solitary, emptied of song.

A few days later I am back in Wales, disconsolate after this brief trip to Rabós. The possibility that I might not return to the village in this lifetime fills me with a creeping sense of dread. I think it has been there, in a silent, wavering form, since the diagnosis of my deteriorated condition, but has been kept at bay by exhaustion, by the fond attentions of my family and, until quite recently by practical issues, especially by my being forced to focus on the launch of my second novel at the end of February. The event, at the Waterstone's bookstore in Cardiff, ran smoothly enough, and there was a good crowd, but I felt listless and unfocused, and was severely underslept, as usual. During the reading, something quite trivial happened, which gives an indication of my beleaguered state of mind. I was speaking to the audience, after the publisher's introduction, about the conception of the novel, when my mobile phone started ringing. My first reaction was one of indignation that on such an occasion it should be me, the reader, who, alone among those present, had failed to switch off his phone. My second thought was more troubling: *if I answer, it will be myself at the other end, wandering the streets, asking where the event is taking place.* I pressed the off button without withdrawing the phone from my pocket. At the reception afterwards, held in a local *tapas* bar, I managed to convey a degree of respectable sanity, even if my movements were a little slow; inside my head, however, lay utter turmoil.

Around this time I receive invitations to travel abroad for overseas editions of my first novel, but have to decline. If I leave the country, I will be suspended from the transplant list for the duration of my absence, which would be foolish, since there is no telling when an appropriate organ might turn up. Now that I have returned to Wales, I will have to stay put, possibly for a long, drawn-out wait: if the wait goes on for many months, and my health deteriorates as expected, I will not be fit enough to withstand the rigours of a transplant operation. A significant proportion of people die before a new organ is found.

Since December, I have been experiencing an unsettling sense of premonition, or rather, pronounced speculation, that this year will be my last, based, reasonably enough, on what I have been told. At Christmas, driving away from my sister's house in the Monmouthshire countryside, after a day spent with my extended family, I felt this speculation swell into a burgeoning certainty; it is an eerie, melancholy emotion, this sense of departure from the people I love, and now, as the months progress, I feel as though I am climbing into an ill-protected fishing launch and battening down the hatches, while around me the storm rages and pilotless oil tankers heave and crash towards me.

5

My earliest memory is of drowning. At around four years of age, either out of forgetfulness, bravado, or a wish to end it all, I jumped into the deep end of a public swimming pool without my rubber ring. My sister Hilary, six years my senior, saw my curly head floating on the surface and thought it was a piece of flotsam that someone had left behind. She swam over to pick it up, and found her youngest brother attached. I was dragged, spluttering and puking, to the side of the pool where my father, who was a doctor, managed to resuscitate me. Jumping into water became a life-long habit.

I was six years old and attended Saint Edmund's Primary School, Crickhowell. Our nearest neighbours were the Evans family, who had a German shepherd called Wolf. Wolf lay outside the entrance to the Evans house and acquired the status of a heroic, mythical beast in my imagination. I was in love with Megan Evans, a beautiful child with long blonde hair and enormous brown eyes. We went haymaking in the Black Mountains in the glorious days of summer, and there, on her uncle's farm, we discovered a barrel of cider that had been left in the barn for the refreshment of the labourers; our heads spinning and little hearts thumping (naked apart from shorts, we took it in turns to listen to each other's pumping chest), we tumbled precociously in the hay before being discovered and disentangled from one another, by one of Megan's bemused aunts. The experience was altogether too pleasant to forget – although, admittedly, the odour of scandal hung over us after being caught, as it were, *in flagrante*, sweetly lubricated subversives of adult authority – and I was driven home and scolded by my mother, who gave me a bath, since I was tipsy and smelled of the farmyard and had straw in my hair. Soon after this, at the age of seven, I was sent away to school, and spent the next ten years in almost exclusively male company. These were the tactics of the moribund British Empire to breed a class of warriors and administrators, and even though my parents did not properly speaking belong to the social class for whom this practice was the norm, I was packed off, like my older brother and sister before me, to a small prep school in

Worcestershire, where my Welsh accent was soon beaten out of me (but not, apparently, my impertinence) and where I excelled in only two pursuits: music and running.

As a child, I was fascinated by stories about haunted woods, hollow trees, and most especially, the ability of sorcerers to manifest themselves as animals. My most treasured book was a green hardcover edition of the Arthurian legends, retold by Barbara Leonie Picard. For a long time, from the age of six, I was terrified by the idea of dying, but could find little reassurance in the things we were told at Sunday school. We were not a religious family, but we went through the motions of church on Sunday. Even as a child my response to Christian doctrine was one of vague astonishment that anyone actually believed the story of the resurrection. As a doctor's son I knew this was impossible. As for the prospect that eternal life awaited us because a benevolent god had chosen to sacrifice his own son for the good of mankind – well this was just plain *wrong*. Surely, I remember thinking, nobody really believes this stuff; surely they are just *pretending* to believe it.

At home, my parents' emotional conduct, not untypically of their generation, was defined by a reserve and sense of decorum that were apparently connected (as was everything else) with "the war", which had ended only a decade before my birth. We endured a collective adherence to a code of non-disclosure, which provoked in me a sense of bewilderment and confusion. I grew up with the received knowledge that any display of feelings was somehow shameful.

The war became a symbol, with time, of difference; the essential divide that marked out our generations. For my parents, nurtured by a regimen that depended on commonality of purpose, the letting down of one's guard indicated a loss of self-control for which one would inevitably suffer; such negligence was almost an extension of the political vicissitudes of wartime, by which careless talk cost lives. In this way the war was given both moral and symbolic capital; it stood for a code of behaviour and of sacrifice. But it also bred in my mother (a Londoner who lived through the Blitz) a sense of survival against the odds and an abhorrence of wastefulness (she famously hung out plastic bags to be re-used, anticipating government recycling programmes by thirty years). My father grew his own vegetables. Thrift and self-sufficiency were ideals to be respected.

But I was often miserable for weeks on end during the school holidays, when my older siblings had moved on and I had no friends in the area. For years I longed to escape that frigid routine of enforced containment and propriety, replicated at home as at school. My misery was alleviated by the annual camping holidays in Italy, France or Spain during the summer holidays, of leaving behind the perennial view of wet slate roofs and setting out down the motorway towards the sun. Adventure appeared as an escape to the south, the Mediterranean, which, as a student of Latin I knew meant 'the centre of the world'.

At the age of twelve, I was entered for a music scholarship to Sherborne School, in Dorset, for which I was required to perform on piano, organ and violin. Music dominated my life, and when I wasn't practising the piano I would run (I started as a sprinter and graduated in my teens to middle-distance). The prospect of this examination took on enormous significance for me as the day approached. My mother drove me down to Dorset and we stayed overnight at the Half Moon Hotel, an old coaching house across from the town's abbey, where throughout the night the chiming of the bells at every quarter of the hour rang through my skull. I was nervous and unsettled, because that night, of all nights, while visiting the bathroom for a pee, I discovered the very first pubic hairs sprouting in what had previously been a smooth, glabrous zone, and the sight both depressed and alarmed me. I felt that something very ugly was happening, over which I had absolutely no control. I wanted to sneak along the corridor and into my mother's room, knowing that if only I could crawl under the blankets with her, I would be able to sleep, like a baby. I was distraught. It was February, the room was icy, and I had no choice but to return to bed and count out the chimes as the old abbey clanged through the small hours until, with the first glimmerings of dawn, I gave up on trying to sleep altogether, and sat up with a book, until my mother called me to get ready for breakfast. When, at the end of that long summer of 1969, term finally began, the whole school experience turned out to be a horrible anti-climax, and I was eventually expelled, after stumbling through four anguished years under the protection – such irony, considering the nature of the man – of a housemaster devoid of any intellectual curiosity whatever, and for whom the sadistic repression of teenage boys' every natural inclination provided the unique criterion for job satisfaction. He was of a type, this man: an Oxford blue, a jock, a chain-smoking, gin-soaked oaf, who had served his country in the war and had returned to Blighty to find that he had no place in normal civilian life, that the world had moved on without him, and that the only option was to be taken back into the protective and infantilising world of the public school system. There were hundreds like him at the time: they were war victims too, in their way, although how these damaged men could be employed as educators now scarcely seems credible.

Sherborne still practised the fagging system, whereby junior boys were obliged to act as personal servants to the prefects, and were frequently selected for their looks, the prettier boys going to the those seniors with a predilection for buggery – whether practised or fantasised. During my first year at Sherborne prefects were also allowed to beat junior boys with a cane. On learning that a friend and I were to be ritually thrashed the next day for some trivial offence – a failure to carry out some aspect of our fagging duties – I convinced my friend, Tim, that we would be better off not attending our morning assignation with the head prefect, and we cycled off in the dead of night to Tim's family home, twelve miles away at Sturminster Newton. When we arrived, we discovered that Tim's father, Sir Arthur Norman, who was Chairman of the CBI at the time, was away dining with Harold Wilson, the prime minister, in Downing Street; but Lady Norman was very sweet, and after listening to our story, told us that we were not to worry, and she promised to speak to her husband that same night. She fed us soup, then bundled us and our bikes into the back of her estate car, returning us to school before dawn, where we climbed the fire escape to our dormitories and grabbed a couple of hours' sleep before the morning bell. Sir Arthur (who also happened to be chairman of the school governors) must have had words with the headmaster early the next morning, because we were not beaten and a contrite and obsequious housemaster called me in after lunch to assure me that any problems I might have should be brought to him, rather than taken into my own hands, and that he would listen with a fair and open mind, and that the castigation from which we fled would not, in fact, take place, nor indeed would there be any punishment as a result of our midnight escapade. He clearly was an idiot not to recognise the inconsistency in his argument: if I had gone to him the day before to confide my worries, nothing would have changed; by acting on my own initiative, on the other hand, I had avoided a thrashing. Nor could I trust him now, knowing that he had acted under pressure from above. But at least our direct action resulted in the banning of corporal punishment by prefects, and brought an end to the fagging system, first in our house, then in the school as a whole. The housemaster and the more antediluvian members of staff never forgave me this act of insubordination.

One Easter, when I was fourteen, my father took me with him on a trip to Athens. We stayed at the Stanley Hotel, on Karaiskaki Square, and we shared a room with two single beds. Every morning I woke to a miracle of bright sunlight, and jumped out of bed, ready for whatever we had planned for that day, since, with my father, there was always a plan to follow. During our week there, we visited most of the essential tourist spots around the capital, and took day trips to Delphi and Mycenae. We climbed Mount Hymaetus where the slopes were crawling with honey-coloured tortoises, and we took a bus to Sounion, from the cliffs of which Theseus's father, Aegeus, hurled himself when he saw that the boat returning his son from Crete bore black sails. I wrote a poem about this, which became my first published piece. I wanted to visit Crete, having discovered a book containing pictures of the Minoan palaces at Knossos and Phaistos. The photographs of Sir Arthur Evans' fantasy palace were reproduced in glossy overwrought colour and the carefully framed shots of eroded temple walls and improbable crimson pillars opened up onto a landscape of orange groves, olive orchards, cypresses, vertiginous snowcapped mountains and an impossibly blue sea. However, the trip to Crete was beyond our budget. A waiter in the

Plaka asked my father if he and I were brothers, which pleased my father. I was less impressed: it seemed rather an obvious ploy.

In the evenings, we sat in the hotel bar before dinner and were served salted almonds with our drinks. It was the first time I tasted fresh almonds. My father, a glutton for punishment, attempted to teach me the rudiments of inorganic chemistry for the exams I was due to take that summer. As the youngest of his three children, I represented the last chance that one of us might follow him into the practice of medicine. His efforts were entirely fruitless, as I was destined to fail the chemistry exam miserably, and do even worse on the re-sit. I was unable, even for a moment, to connect the chemical formulae I was being taught with any aspect of experienced reality; nor was my curiosity stimulated, the only basis for me wanting to study anything. I lost concentration from the moment he began his explanations, and my mind wandered, focusing on anything but chemistry: the way the waiter flirted with a female guest, the cut of a man's suit (not the British style), the ceaseless flow of traffic far below. It was an exasperating task for my father, confronted, as he must have been, by my expression of glazed incomprehension.

Greece was ruled by the Colonels' Dictatorship. I didn't know who the Colonels were, but according to my father they were a pretty bad lot. The morning before we left, I went out from the hotel early, before breakfast, in order to buy something, perhaps a gift for my mother. I was returning to the hotel when a car careened around the roundabout at Omonia, scattering a storm of political flyers in its wake, a thousand red sheets, then took off with a screech of burning tyres. It took a minute for the police to get there, sirens blaring. One car skidded to the kerb beside me. A plain-clothes man in shades got out, a snub-nosed submachine gun dangling at his hip, picked up a clutch of flyers, stuffed one in his coat, turned and gobbed towards the sun. When the car was gone, I had to look. His spittle streaked the pavement, specked with blood and something else, which looked alive. I turned for the hotel. A gust of wind lifted a few of the flyers into the air, circling, dipping, blown like autumn leaves, rising on the thermals, flakes of scarlet against the deepening blue, with the Acropolis behind.

I composed music for the school production of Macbeth, and conducted the small orchestra, as well as writing a clarinet sonata, a wind trio, pieces for viola and piano, and a string quartet. For two summers I attended the European Summer School for Young Musicians, which took place, one year, near Lausanne in Switzerland, and the next at Caen in Normandy. At the Swiss school I played in the percussion section of the orchestra alongside the young Simon Rattle, and I attended composition classes. My pieces were later performed at concerts in the school hall or in Sherborne Abbey. This – along with my success as a middle-distance runner – gained me a certain respectability, which I lacked elsewhere, but my love of music was gradually overtaken by an immersion in literature. I had always written poems and stories, but from around fifteen or sixteen, literature became a more obsessive pursuit. My school work thrived under the guidance of a gentle and quietly inspirational teacher called Lionel Bruce, and I read widely, far beyond the curriculum. Among the poets taught by Lionel I liked Eliot, but preferred Pound, enjoyed the metaphysicals, especially Donne and Marvell. I was introduced to the major themes of German Romanticism by Timothy Garton Ash, who was a couple of years my senior, and I read Schopenhauer, the philosopher of anguished young men, and Nietzsche, Thomas Mann and Herman Hesse, and listened to Wagner and Mahler with him in a rather grimy orange-painted music room at the school. It was Tim who surprised me a couple of years later, outside the Bodleian, by telling me that while at school he had considered me the embodiment of negative capability, an expression I assumed to be insulting and had to look up. I read extensively, devouring the fiction of Dostoyevsky, Kafka, Joyce, Hamsun, Miller, Genet, Burroughs and the Beats, although Kerouac I found rambling and sentimental.

I was seventeen when I changed my mind about becoming a composer and decided I wanted to write instead. It came about quite specifically through the discovery of a short story called 'The Lion', by a little-known writer and sculptor, Christoph Meckel, in a collection of contemporary German writing. This melancholy and magical story, about a solitary man who befriends a lion, unravelled for me the need for fiction to adhere to any single received understanding of reality, a notion that I found compelling, and it became for me a kind of paradigm of what can be achieved in two or three pages of prose.

When I was eventually expelled from Sherborne – specifically for the Socratic crime of exercising a corrupting influence on the younger boys – I spent the few remaining months before my A levels in Oxford, where I attended what used to be called a crammer (in fact a dumping ground for the myriad rejects of the private education system) and arrangements were made for me to have tutorials with postgraduate students from the university. It was while studying in Oxford that I got to know a young French woman, Isabelle Kahan, who was working as a gardener in The Parks. Isabelle went back to Paris before I took my exams, but she told me I would be welcome to visit her, whenever I should choose to visit France.

I decided that if I was to become a writer I should avoid reading English Literature at university, since I had picked up the notion – I have no idea whether it was spontaneous or something I had heard and affected to believe – that the study of literary criticism was death to any budding writer. Besides, Oxford was full of precisely the kind of people I went to school with and needed to get away from. I wanted to study anthropology, and the best place to do that, as well as being the coolest place to go – as it was the only university at which a death had occurred during the recent wave of student protests – was the London School of Economics. I had plenty of time before then, however, as I planned to spend a year working and travelling.

6

Night is falling. From my study window I watch a train pull out from Cardiff Central and I wait, without knowing quite what for. The literature from the hospital Liver Unit tells of 'waiting for the call', yet it does not feel like waiting in any sense that I am familiar with. In waiting for an event which might be life-threatening, and whose outcome is unknown, the waiting itself becomes the process of existing, a seemingly interminable attendance on a Godot whose configuration is as obscure as death itself.

The episodes of encephalopathy are becoming the story of my life. This is what they mean by people being defined by their illness. I am in danger of becoming little more than the vessel of my ruined liver. And in the meantime I'm going off my trolley.

Since the onset of brain fog, I have become profoundly distanced from the obstacle course of the world outside this house. This has happened, by stages, almost without my noticing. More accurately, it is as if a protective bubble separated me from the real world and, as I go out less and less, when I do venture into town, or take the dog for a walk in the park, I do not experience life directly, but as if through an invisible intermediary, walking alongside me. Or else I notice things only at the periphery of my vision, witness figures slipping slowly down the knotted rope that sways above an uncharted chasm. The other night, unable to sleep, as always, but incapable also of reading, of watching a DVD, or of writing, I decided, at four in the morning, to visit the all-night supermarket in the Bay. I could do the weekly grocery shop, I thought, that would save an extra job, and occupy me for an hour or so. I took the car, and stopping at lights by the bridge across the river, was hailed by a prostitute who was approaching the crossing from my right. A single man, driving around a zone frequently patrolled by members of her profession at such an hour, it is only reasonable of her to assume I might be a potential client. I recognise her: I have seen her before. She has an easier, friendlier manner than most of her fellow workers, perhaps she is more confident on account of her good looks, and she is young, though not outrageously so, not like some of the pubescent vampires that haunt the neighbourhood streets. Her face has a certain intelligence about it also, and I think that she reminds me of a woman I once knew, though who knows whether I believed such a terrible cliché at the time or have made it up since; at least her eyes, even from the distance of twenty paces, did not have the frozen-fish glaze of so many of her smacked-out colleagues. Because my gaze meets hers, momentarily, she hurries her pace towards the car, just as the lights change, and I pull away.

Being inside a car, inside a moving object with windows, is a well-worn but precise analogy for the way I was feeling, the protective bubble sensation. Perhaps, though, the car exaggerates the sense of desolation I feel when I glimpse the forcing of a smile on the woman's face, a smile that, for that brief instant appears entirely *unforced* – and again I blame my excitable imagination – as if she has recognised a kindred spirit rather than merely a potential client (why do we hunger so for kindred spirits?) as she hastens her steps towards my car, seconds before I accelerate, with such an invasive sense of sadness for her, for the riverside wasteland I am driving through, the haze of illuminated rain in my headlamps, for the world my own daughters, safe in their beds, will soon inherit, for my regret at so many wrong moves in the past, for the indecipherable future. When I get to the supermarket, I wander the aisles in a state of suspended but almost crippling despair, selecting goods with placid concentration, there in the almost deserted superstore in which one can purchase not only food, but clothes, computers, microwave ovens, lottery tickets. I lean heavily on my trolley, with that dull, relentless pain in my side, my feet and ankles swollen with oedema, and by the time I have finished several circuits of the aisles it is seven o'clock and I have spent three hours in this semi-comatose state, here in this tacky emporium of useless goods, with the supermarket radio station playing bad pop, occasionally breaking off to inform me of special offers on pre-cooked chickens or electrical appliances. When I return home my daughters are finishing their breakfast, preparing to leave for school, and only here, safely back with my loved ones, does the bubble begin to dissolve. I stretch out on the sofa, Bruno the puppy tries to get up with me and wash my face, but I push him away and he lies down on the floor, lifting his head occasionally to try and lick my hand. What goes through a dog's head? How I envy him his benign ignorance.

7

Our sense of the passage of time itself accelerates with the passing of time, since each day, week or year constitutes a smaller percentage of the overall sum of days, weeks, years that have been lived. And yet, of course, this is a purely subjective experiencing of time, an effect of our having become accustomed to our routines, and the moment we step outside routine, break our quotidian habits, embark on a new adventure, or suffer from chronic insomnia, we experience time differently; we may indeed find that time slows up, and begins to resume a tempo familiar to us from childhood, when the hours would stretch ahead into infinity.

Dipping into Montaigne's *Travel Journal*, an account of a journey the author made to Switzerland in 1580, we find that in a churchyard, at Neufchâteau, the gravestones are inscribed with a peculiar phrase: *Here lies so-and-so, who was dead when time was passing through the year twelve hundred.* That time is itself personified, is conceived of in this fashion, as though it were an active agent, *passing through*, runs in contradiction to the idea, or metaphor, that we are the active agents on a journey *through time,* and this paradox is difficult to sustain, is even shocking, at least to twenty-first century sensibilities.

We are familiar with expressions that rely on the personification of time, such notions as 'time waits for no one': we accept the cliché without hesitation, just as we can easily conceive of something as a 'waste of time' or try to 'save time' by doing a task in a certain way rather than another (which might involve us wasting even more time); all three expressions are metaphors, of course, but we do not question the notion that, figuratively speaking, we are on a journey, and the idea that 'time is on the move' is also a commonplace. Yet the notion that 'the year twelve hundred' might be a static entity, *through which time passes*, is a novel one to me. Perhaps it accurately represents a medieval world-view. If an acceptance of predestination was prevalent among believers at the time, then clearly everything would be mapped out in advance, and although people did not know the outcome of their lives in advance, God did: every hair of the head was numbered, every action had a foreseen consequence, and everyone had their destiny. So the year 1200 came and went, *time passed through,* it followed the course that had been determined for it, by God, and so-and-so died. This conceptualisation of time left nothing to chance, or even to choice, since even apparently autonomous decisions were circumscribed by a terrible, all-embracing determinism.

Insomnia allows us a chink in the armour of time. Since we are accustomed to the division of time into identifiable segments, which we measure as hours and days and weeks, we can measure the pace of our passage through time quite conveniently, but once that structure begins to break down, once the notion of 'time passing' over hours and days is exposed as a convenient fiction, everything begins to look rather different.

One of the first things the chronic insomniac notices is an inability to keep track of the days. Since one's life is a continuum of sleeplessness, snatching rare hours here and there at random times of the day or night, yesterday seeps into tomorrow without allowing today to get a toehold.

Another aspect of insomnia, at least in my case, is *slowness.* Rose has remarked on the fact that my movements, my speech, have slowed considerably over the past few months. We know that cirrhosis causes loss of appetite, fatigue and muscle wastage; this last would account for the thinning of my arms while the legs remain swollen with oedema, causing me to resemble a childhood ghost, a character called Mr Wobbly Man: a somewhat tragic figure who used to appear in the Noddy stories of Enid Blyton, and who could not lie down. It also causes tiredness of the eyes, and a deterioration in my vision, and I am certain that my reactions have slowed. But these are physical phenomena and what I am referring to is *ontological* slowness, slowness of being, slowness of perception, slowness of thought, slowness of speech. Time, it seems, has slowed up for me, and the days are not easily measured. I forget things constantly. I recall something as having happened several days earlier, of having met so-and-so in the park during my morning walk, possibly someone real, or a so-and so I have pilfered from my reading of Montaigne or retained from a dream, and my daughters tell me, to the contrary, that what I am describing happened only this morning, and I have already told them.

8

At seventeen I set off for Paris and met up with Isabelle, who had blue eyes, wore a gipsy headscarf and impressive earrings, even had a gold tooth. She was six years older than me, and had been a student at Nanterre, where the events of 1968 first ignited. Isabelle was a revolutionary: she had stood at the Paris barricades alongside Daniel Cohn-Bendit and Guy Debord. For me, she held all the romantic appeal of that May, tinged with a surrealist poetry that demanded the impossible, had flowers blooming beneath paving stones, and exhortations to open the windows of one's heart and to destroy the society of the spectacle. Isabelle's father, a one-legged Russian émigré, had been a war hero, a general in the Free French and colleague of de Gaulle. He was a formidable chess player and his obsession with the game, which I also played – with a recklessness that dismayed the general – provided an excuse for him to tolerate my rather scurrilous affair with his daughter. We played chess for hours every day, and he bellowed angrily at Isabelle when she interrupted us to take me out for the evening. However, in spite of the general's happiness at finding a chess partner, the family had standards to maintain, and rather than being allowed to stay in their cramped suburban apartment, Isabelle and I were dispatched to the southwest, where we spent the summer in a ruined farmhouse her parents had recently bought, overlooking the River Lot.

Isabelle was a spontaneously joyful person, who made friends easily. She found us work on a neighbouring farm belonging to a communist party activist, Emile. We picked peaches and aubergines – a foretaste, under extremely benign conditions, of my future career as an agricultural labourer – and one night we trailed through the local villages with our employer and one of his comrades in his old Renault van, sticking Communist Party posters on any available wall-space, an activity that Isabelle and I participated in with a degree of scepticism. If only they knew my father was a general, whispered Isabelle. But on being told that Emile's friend was suffering from depression after separating from his wife, we lent a hand out of compassionate solidarity.

Isabelle, apart from delivering an extremely thorough education in sexual matters, taught me how to cook ratatouille, how to make peach jam – this was less successful than the ratatouille, turning to a mildly alcoholic gloop within a week – and introduced me to three French writers who would open up new worlds to me: Villon, Rimbaud and Céline. She also had an autobiography by a Cretan novelist, Constantinos Kazantzakis' *Report to Greco*, and had been to Crete herself. She rekindled my enthusiasm for the island by telling me stories of her travels there.

We had the farmhouse to ourselves for most of the summer, and after a long day in the fields, we would return home to ratatouille and lots of red wine and we would do it: we did it on the kitchen table, or in the neighbour's barn, or in the tool shed next to the neighbour's barn, or in the maize field under the warm rain, or in the woods down by the River Lot, or on the flat roof-terrace, or in front of the log fire, or we would take our blankets and a candle outside and lie under the stars and Isabelle would read to me from Villon and Rimbaud, which always evoked a sense of swimming through language, stroking through the warm, dense lubrications of the French with an unhurried pleasure, and an excited anticipation for the fulfilment of sensuous journeys whose destinations I could barely imagine, but of which I was guaranteed at least a foretaste through Isabelle's passionate ministrations.

Just before my eighteenth birthday, Isabelle's mother drove down from Paris for a few days to oversee some building work on the house, and she bought me as a present an old piano accordion from a junk shop in Porte-Sainte-Marie. The accordion wheezed asthmatically, but I quickly mastered the basics and in the long evenings of the Gascon summer, after eating on the patio, I churned out waltzes and polkas while Isabelle and her mother danced in an unsteady embrace around the jasmine-scented garden. I also wrote a number of poems and songs, accompanying myself on the guitar, predictably mournful compositions on the whole, influenced by Leonard Cohen and The Velvet Underground. The general too paid a visit for a few days in August, and once again his passion for chess got the better of his sense of disapproval. I was committed to three hours of chess every evening. One Sunday afternoon we all went swimming in a nearby lake, and

I was amazed to see the general slip off his prosthetic leg, arse-shuffle down the little beach, and flop into the water like a seal. He pushed off, his one leg splashing, and once he had reached the centre of the lake flipped onto his back, and, to the embarrassment of his children, and the bewilderment of the local picnickers, began to sing, extremely loudly, in Russian.

Isabelle wrote an amorous dedication on the title page of her well-thumbed paperback edition of Rimbaud's poems – minus half its cover, fecklessly appropriated for roach material – and presented it to me when I left. I travelled with it for years, before it was destroyed in a general bonfire of my possessions in the Peloponnese. For years, too, I carried with me the sound of her whispered incantation *"on n'est pas sérieux, quand on a dix-sept ans"*, in a voice that could not help sounding salacious, even while mouthing innocent endearments.

9

Recently, I have begun wearing an expression of stoned incomprehension in public places, and strangers, especially shopkeepers, often assume that I am either drunk or mentally deficient. I fumble for change, unable to coordinate my fingers, my language gets confused, I swear inappropriately as though suffering from Tourette's; knowing that someone is surveying me in the certainty that I must be drunk, I feel frustrated, and even, on occasions, affronted. My family knows that this laboriously slow and slurred conduct is a part of my condition, but for strangers I have the demeanour of either a moron or a piss-head. The other night I had to go to the garage to buy cigarettes (another habit that is supposed to harm one's ability to sleep. I have given up for long periods – it has never been difficult for me to give up smoking – but my sleep has not improved): it was around three in the morning and the garage is often quite busy at this time of night, taxi drivers re-fuel there and revellers returning from the bars and nightclubs often congregate, night-birds, assorted lowlife, would-be muggers, miscellaneous criminal and otherwise unsavoury types. The filling-station service counter is staffed at night by an Asian man with a fundamentalist beard, his English is very poor, or maybe it is my language that is incomprehensible to him, because he stares at me with poorly-concealed disgust, I *know* he thinks I am drunk, and he demonstrates a stubborn refusal to understand my words when I request a certain brand of cigarettes, makes a clicking sound with his tongue, and asks me to repeat myself, which I do, with no success. The man is losing patience, and a queue is forming behind me. I try again, forming the syllables slowly, making sure I do not slur my words. But something goes wrong, whether it is my enunciation, or his lack of English, or the buzzing of insects on the night air, or the roar of an unforeseen tsunami rising over Cardiff Bay, or the barrier presented by the reinforced glass panel through which we must speak – since this is a night-service counter, designed to protect the attendant from the violent assaults of his customers, I cannot be sure, but I sense we are in a situation of communicative meltdown. As my frustration grows, so too does the muffled sound of complaint from those waiting behind me. I turn to snarl at them; how ridiculous, I am looking for a fight now, I want my cigarettes and everything else has receded into a fog, I am livid that this bastard cannot understand a word I am saying, so I turn around to face a triumvirate of young Somalis in hoodies, no doubt harbingers of random urban retribution, and I envision myself, a few seconds hence, curled in a puddle on the dark tarmac, shielding my head from the blows and kicks that pummel my body, sniffing back blood and snot and tears. Then one of them catches my eye and his face lights up and he flicks back his hood: Hey, man, and he beams at me. I have no idea who he is. You remember me, man? Ahmed, you taught me English. When I first come over. Everything tight wiv you, bro? Need help or somefing?

I look him in the face: a handsome, smiling boy. He seems concerned, anxious to be of assistance. Sudden clarity: this young man was one of a clutch of Somali child refugees who arrived in the wake of the civil war in 1991. I taught a small class of six, when I worked for the City Council English Language Service, under Ravi Mooneram, all those years ago. He was a good kid, they all were, they had come from hell, they had been bombed by their own air force, starved, beaten, in some cases seen their parents murdered, and now here he was in Grangetown, no doubt having benefited from a few years of inadequate education and a further spell at finishing school in the Grangetown Badboy Academy for young offenders, and here, at this miserable filling station under the persistent drizzle of Welsh rain, years on, he has come to rescue me. His two friends gather round. All three insist on shaking my hand. Hi, I say, nice to meet you Ahmed, after all these years, you think you can help me out here? Blue Camel and some chocolate, any chocolate. My tongue has apparently awakened. I give him a ten pound note and step back from the wretched serving hole. Sure, man, says Ahmed, and I look away, I've had enough of trying with the hatchet-faced, humourless man at the till, and I hear Ahmed do the business in strangulated Cardiff hip-hop: Gissum camel man, da blue, and a Ga-lax-ee. He insists on counting out all the change and, as I walk off, I wonder at the perversity of a world in which he, whom I helped to speak the language, should have to translate for me.

10

After saving money from a job on a building site, I left for Crete, not with Isabelle, but with an old school friend, Nigel Douglas, who was going up to Cambridge later that year to read English. After descending through Italy and taking the ferry from Brindisi to Igoumenitsa, we travelled across mainland Greece and the Cretan sea, landing in Iraklion one morning in May. We studied the map, and on the perfectly rational basis of its reputation as the centre of banana cultivation on the island, made for the southern village of Arvi. There followed a month's ruthless exploitation at the hands of a banana farmer, Fat Manoli, who bore a keen resemblance to a well-known American TV cop. The temperature soared in the heat of the day as we weeded between the trees, and the air stank of the rotting trunks of dead banana plants, but Fat Manoli was not inclined to offer us breaks. We used chicken shit for fertiliser, and humped huge bulging sacks from the truck to the trees – which in itself was no great problem – but the nature of the work inevitably meant that one acquired cuts and grazes, and the chicken shit always found its way into these abrasions and stung like hell.

One day we took a hike along the coast to the west of the village. After an hour or so we came upon a long golden beach which stretched far into the distance. We stopped for a swim and afterwards, on impulse, I scrambled to the top of the steep sandy cliff that overlooked the beach. Arriving at the crest, I noticed a stone hut that lay a little further back and which was not visible from below. There was a doorless entry to the small building, a single room with evidence that one corner had once served as a fireplace, an earthen floor and a roof of tightly bound thatch. The place seemed entirely abandoned.

We moved in, after returning to Arvi to collect our things and stock up on provisions. We had saved some money from the job with Fat Manoli, as well as still having a little money of our own. We needed to find a water source, as the stream that ran along the gorge behind the hut was dry, and I did not yet know the landscape well enough to hunt for wells. The hillside was covered with brushwood and heather, and we collected armfuls for bedding: it made a soft mattress when covered with a blanket. The hut became our hide-out. It did not feel as though we were intruding on someone else's home – the hut was clearly not in use as a shepherd's refuge; there was no livestock in sight for miles around, apart from the occasional tethered goat at farm buildings on the village outskirts, an hour away. However, we soon discovered another tiny settlement at half an hour's leisurely walk to the west, by the name of Keratokambos, also the name of the mountain below which it stood. There we found a *kafeneion*, where we could buy raki, wine and canned food, and a well, which considerably shortened the water run. The owner was a handsomely weathered man, the most laid-back, imperturbable and idle of hosts. He spent most of the day either asleep in a chair, or, when the arduous nature of sitting upright overpowered him, on a hammock shaded by the vines that covered the patio. We ordered a carafe of raki and passed the afternoons playing games of chess in this cool arbour as the surf pounded the shore behind us. Then, in the early evening, the villagers would start to congregate on the café patio to watch the village's only television (TV was a recent arrival in the south of Crete) and, taking turns to shoulder the demijohn of fresh water, we made our way back to the hut, and enjoyed the spectacle of sunset as gradually the sky darkened and the mountains behind us turned blue, then deep violet. We prepared our fire and cooked a meal of fish and potatoes and sat outside the hut, absorbed in the enveloping night and the sound of the sea below us.

These were magical evenings, and in our wine-flushed talk we would have sounded earnest and unforgiving, armed with our arrogance, our meagre talent and fantastic dreams; we were steeped in ideas and the pleasure of a seemingly infinite amount of time in which to mull them over, turn them inside out, argue, proclaim, discuss works of literature. I read Dostoyevsky's *Brothers Karamazov* there, along with Mann's *Magic Mountain*. I read Nabokov's early novels, *The Defence* and *The Gift*, translated from the Russian, but most importantly, it was here that I discovered the *Fictions* of Borges, which I had in the Calder and Boyars edition, revelations in the art of condensed narrative and circumspect wit, which I read and re-read, with the realisation that this was what I had been looking for, this was the writer I had been seeking. I was utterly won over by Borges, his stories entranced me, suspending me for days on end in a state of excitement about the transformative powers of great writing.

Late in July, Nigel – who did not share my enthusiasm for Borges – returned to England, and coming back from Iraklion, where I had gone to see him off on the ferry, I found, to my surprise, that someone had paid a visit to my hut. Lying in the entrance was a bottle of the purest 'proto' raki and a box of *loukoumi* (Turkish delight), bound with a coarse ribbon. I was at a loss as to who might have delivered such a gift. I had never seen anyone in the vicinity of the hut. The mystery was resolved a couple of days later when a lithe, elderly Cretan appeared as I sat reading outside the little house. He was, he told me, the owner of the place, but had no use for it, and was most welcoming, telling me I could stay there for as long as I wished. This man helped to form, or corroborate an existent model, of the best type of Greek male: enigmatic, generous, with that proclivity for laughter, a sense of humour based on paradox and the surreal, that is peculiarly Greek (no doubt he found my squatting in his hut fairly surreal: this was before the invasion of mass tourism that occurred over the next decade). I brewed coffee for this guest who was also my host, and conversed in pidgin Greek, illustrated with gesticulation and mime. His was the only visit I received while living there, at least until Paula, a gloriously uninhibited girlfriend from Crawley – and a dead ringer for the young Sissy Spacek in *Badlands* – turned up. Her arrival changed the nature of my relationship to the place completely and my experiment with the hermit's life came to an end.

I stayed two months in the shepherd's hut at the foot of Keratokambos. I discovered something that has coloured my perception, infiltrated my dreams and influenced my thought ever since: practically everywhere you go on this island you are walking on the remains of an earlier civilisation, a buried and lost world beneath your feet. Every footfall creates an echo that rebounds around the nearby gorge, and that might, conceivably, be heard in another age, another epoch. Do the ghosts of the subterranean world hear the ghosts of the future shuffling the stones and the dirt somewhere above them? Is this, by a circuitous correlation, why some of us feel compelled to write? Are we trying, somehow, to transcend the boundaries of time, to write in the face of a fixed chronology, knowing that the hardest thing on earth would be to find the right words to conjure a particular instance of time passing, even as an invasive silence spreads onto the screen, bewildering in its glacial white? This is the silence engendered by the writer's sense of *hubris*, and yet the only thing more overwhelming than this resistance to writing is the compulsion to write.

Of that summer, I remember more than anything else the mornings when I was there alone. I rose early, gathered a towel, scrambled down the cliff for a swim, and returned in time to catch the solar wind, an event I had never encountered before. As the sun rose over the sea to the east on an otherwise still and breezeless morning, a powerful draft of warm air would blow across the hillside, lifting the scent of wild thyme in its wake, always on cue, a mysterious and portentous welcome to the day, an event I looked forward to each morning: something so primordial, cleansing and invigorating, like a total absolution in nature, and a surrender to the sun, which is, of course, the primary manifestation of God.

I have encountered the solar wind on different occasions since then, in other places, but never has it been as overwhelming or magical as in Crete, and always, when I feel it, I am returned to that hillside shack under the horned mountain.

11

Tonight, at around two o'clock, sleepless, I go downstairs, make tea, and settle in front of a television movie in which giant carnivorous spiders are decimating a small Midwestern community. I return to the kitchen and swallow a sleeping pill, even though I doubt the wisdom or the efficacy of such a gesture. I take another for good measure, return to the sofa, and the film. The spiders are having a ball with the slow-witted inhabitants of what is now Webville, USA. I watch without joy as a citizen is injected with spider venom, wrapped in spider silk and tossed in the county jail by an enterprising arachnid. I switch the television to mute and slide a disk into the CD player, music by a woman whose voice reminds me of drowning birds, but the acuity of emotion is unbearable and after three songs I eject and opt for Bach fugues, played by a Russian pianist with almost pathological exactitude. For a short while, there is no conflict between the need for sleep and the requirement of this music for absolute precision of thought.

When the music stops, they come back to me, the voices of the absent and the lost, friends, lovers, the sounds they make muffled by the persistent thrum of my insomnia, straining across the divide between life and the abyss; ghosts lurking at the peripheries of thought, at the borders of the imaginable, before night sucks them back into infinity, to which access is limited only to the briefest and most subtle of glances.

At such times the visual sense is always secondary: it is the sounds these phantoms make that stay in the memory, the words they enunciate, uttering phrases borrowed or purloined from their lifetimes, and if there is an image it is most often a barely significant gesture, a movement of the head or hand, perhaps one that escaped my notice or that I took for granted when I knew a particular voice's owner as a living, human form, a gesture mutely expressing desire or need or complaint or indignity or sudden inexplicable joy or longing, or fear or sadness or grief; or quite simply nothing, nothing at all, no gesture, no imprecation, just a whisper, a single word, that is the most heartrending, a word, or a name, spoken in sorrow. A word, a single word, or sometimes a cluster of words, in a sequence that can elicit heartbreak or fury, nostalgia or silence.

Will you come with me to Santorini?
I know your secret.
The world is blue, like an orange.

How easily assailable seems the cardboard fortress that we build around our frantic, insular lives; how fragile the defences that we throw together against the inevitability of our joining them, the departed. It is as though we only need to push lightly against a transparent screen, to test the spongy surface of the things we take for granted, our daily furnishing of that specious sense of a single well-rehearsed reality, and everything, the whole insane parade of life, will disappear, and we shall be left confounded, desolate, wandering again, or more exactly, in my own case, pacing the floor of my study, the rooms of this house, descending to the kitchen, climbing the stairs again to my lofty, silent outpost, where sleep eludes me for such protracted spells of time that I am left craving it desperately, whether that sleep is temporary or permanent, it barely seems to matter, it barely seems to make a difference.

I have never been to Santorini, and it is unlikely that I will go now. Nor am I likely to visit Zanzibar, or the Himalayas, or the forests of Yucatán.

12

The incident returns to me with a start as I retrace that summer of 1975 in my memory. I was returning from Crete with Paula, and we had stopped off in Venice. Paula was eighteen and I had recently celebrated my nineteenth birthday. We had been travelling all day. I seem to recall we had been arguing, in any case we were fed up and tired. She had a slim boyish body, luxurious long red hair and pink nipples. We didn't really know each other that well but we shared something raw and vital and were good together. We had met a couple of times in England, slept together once, and she had come over to visit me in Crete, hardly a measured decision. She was a gambler, Paula. After Crete we had gone to Athens, then taken the long, boring coach trip through Yugoslavia. We sat in a café and watched the last boat cutting through the waters of the Grand Canal. It was just past midnight and there would not be any more public transport. We had begun looking for a hostel, but the prices were inflated. Venice was expensive and smelly and hot. This didn't bother me too much, but Paula was in a strop. I walked over to the bar and asked about a cheap hotel. One of the customers, a man in his fifties, smartly dishevelled, a maroon shirt, red eyes that were lined with kohl, took up my question, placed an arm around my shoulder, led me back to the table where Paula sat and sulked. He admired Paula's magnificent hair, something which she had become used to in Greece. The waiter followed us with three glasses of a faintly bitter dessert wine. Paula perked up: there was a different scent on the air, perhaps the man's perfume, perhaps simply danger. He was drunk, but upright and coherent: not obsequiously friendly, not overbearing, and there was something distinctly seedy about him.

You do not need to pay for a hostel, he told us. I live nearby and have a large apartment. I live alone. You can sleep there. You can make love. No one will disturb you. You can make love all night long.

We were apparently unwilling to dwell on the perversity of this invitation or of any number of unsavoury contingencies that might await us: of unwittingly participating in a porn movie, or even a snuff movie; of being sold into slavery; of being drugged and made to perform in a sado-masochistic sex ritual before being stabbed and dumped in a canal. When I whispered these possible outcomes in her ear (adopting the lubricious growl of a sex fiend) as we walked along, Paula only giggled. We followed the man, who was now singing gently in a rather fine tenor voice, along labyrinthine alleys and over a dozen narrow bridges. It was all very reminiscent of *Don't Look Now,* which had come out a couple of years earlier. Anything for a bed, sighed Paula, and squeezed my hand. She seemed quite light-headed. Perhaps our drinks had been spiked. Besides, she said, I am not afraid. You will protect me; in the event of any caddish or improper advances on my person, you will strike him down with your mighty sword, you manly man.

With such an endorsement, what could I do? We followed the stranger, and once inside his building we climbed to the first floor. The apartment was large, palatial even. Our host showed us our bedroom. There were clean sheets on the bed. I saw how drunk and lonely the man was. He was almost in tears. You sleep here, he nodded. *Fate amore.* We were tired and the world suddenly seemed very old, and the turn of events perfectly scripted, so that night we made love in his bed, and then we slept. I had always been a light sleeper. No one disturbed us. There was no tippy-toeing in the long corridor, no suspect sounds of shuffling or heavy breathing by the door. Paula woke once in the night, clutched my arm, gasped, and fell back into the pillows. It was a dream: *nothing,* she said, still asleep, when I asked her what was wrong, *it's nothing.*

In the morning, I wandered down the corridor. The bathroom was steamy from a recent shower. On returning to the bedroom, I passed the kitchen. I saw the man through the open door. He was dressed in clean clothes: grey suit and a pressed shirt and purple tie. He gestured me in. He was tearing the plastic cap from a bottle of vermouth. A saucer lay in front of him on the table; on it, I swear, was a single bulbous eye. He offered me a drink, but I declined. I went to wake Paula. It had suddenly become imperative to get out of the man's house.

13

One afternoon I receive a phone call, asking if I would be interested in writing an article to commemorate the centenary of Archie Cochrane, a well known epidemiologist, a curious combination of the scientist and the romantic, a man in many ways epitomising, and yet at conflict with, his times. I would not normally have considered such a project, but I discover that Cochrane (about whom I know next to nothing) was linked to the two locations where I spend most of my life: south Wales and Catalunya, as well as (although in a more incidental way) to the island of Crete, where I lived, on and off, for several years. My curiosity is further stimulated, when, as so often occurs on first encountering a new word or name, that same afternoon I come across a reference to Cochrane in the book I happen to be reading, Anthony Beevor's study of *Crete: the battle and the resistance.* He tells of a troop of Spanish Republicans, survivors of their country's civil war, who were attached to the beleagured British army on Crete in 1941. How these Spaniards came to be in Crete itself constitutes a fascinating story. Refugees in France, following Franco's victory, and shut away in camps under appalling conditions, they had volunteered for the French foreign service battalions and been posted to Syria. When Syria became a part of Vichy France, they left for Palestine, then a British Mandated Territory, and signed up to serve in the British army. There, they were allocated to Layforce, a commando outfit, consisting of four battalions, of which one, D Battalion, contained around seventy of their number: "For the Spanish Republicans, the prospect of capture was especially grim. The Germans would almost certainly return them to Franco's Spain where they would be shot like all the other Republicans they had handed over, from militiamen to former ministers in the Popular Front government. Fortunately, the battalion medical officer, Captain Cochrane, who had served in Spain with the International Brigades, had the idea that they should pretend to be Gibraltarians when interrogated."

My wife's family were Andalucians from La Linea, in the province of Cadiz, who escaped Franco's cavalry by fleeing to Gibraltar in

1936, and who similarly adopted a switch of affiliation, becoming 'Gibraltarians' on their arrival in Britain at the end of World War Two. I became intrigued by the story of these lost Republicans. I imagined that they would have found it much easier to adapt to the conditions in Crete than the Tommies did. Battered units of men, British, Australian and New Zealander, staggered through the olive groves, paralytic on looted wine and raki, skin blistering in the unforgiving sun, feet in shreds from tramping the inhospitable terrain, dodging patrols of the pursuing German paratroopers. Beevor says that during the chaotic retreat across the mountains of Crete, the Spanish proved themselves to be the most experienced foragers. Even Evelyn Waugh, who, like Cochrane, was attached (as the brigade intelligence officer) to Layforce – and who went on to write his own account of the battle of Crete in his novel *Officers and Gentlemen* – apparently relaxed his pro-Franco prejudices when invited by the Republicans to share their spit-cooked sucking pig. (Waugh was a renowned glutton, so it is hardly surprising that he put his belly before his principles. His son Auberon recorded how, at the end of rationing in Britain, each family was allocated one banana per child. These exotic objects were unknown on the home front in wartime, and had acquired the fabulous mystique that only the unattainable can bestow. The Waugh children sat around the table salivating, in a state of famished anticipation, as portly Papa Evelyn, knife and fork in hand, napkin tucked into his stiff collar, demolished all three of the succulent fruit that had been allocated to his offspring, topping off his meal with cream and sugar, also heavily rationed at the time).

I have already mentioned how my own generation differed from the one directly preceding it and, even more so, from the generation of *their* parents, who grew up under Queen Victoria. There seems to be a consensus that this divide is marked most dramatically by the decade of the sixties, in which I was a child, when the attitudes and mores of a post-war culture underwent a seismic shift towards the empowerment of youth and what became known as youth culture, setting new paradigms, marking out new territories for the young. But, as I have pointed out, my generation started off in the frugal shadow of their war, the Second World War, and received by osmosis the need to shoulder some of the austerity and sense of survival against the odds that our parents had experienced. As a child, when we drove down to our capital city, Cardiff, traces of the war were on open display, the bombed-out docklands and parts of the city centre still an eyesore. I grew up with an inexplicable feeling that something was missing, that some expectation, never clearly defined or elaborated, needed to be fulfilled, not simply (although this too occurred to me) as though any moment now the sirens might start, or that, glancing from the bedroom window, I might witness the plummeting descent of a doodlebug, but a sensation of absence, a void, or a feeling of the relative frivolity of our times, which became replaced, in adolescence, by a typically youthful (but in my case, entirely excessive) experimentation with danger of one kind or another, and the inevitable riot of extreme behaviour that accompanies it. Maybe this is what young men do, with variation, around the globe, when they have no satisfactory rituals of initiation into adulthood, or when the rituals on offer are inadequate, abusive and anachronistic (I, of course, went to a school in which they were all three).

Whatever the cause, I experienced a hunger for danger, for seeking out the edge of things. It took me years to figure out what it was I lacked, why I had inherited this appalling sense of mission, but I believe now that it was largely because young men of my generation had no war to go to. I am not, by this, expressing the opinion, or offering a solution, suggesting that this is how things should be, but because of the precedent of the two generations before us, because of the context in which we grew up, inundated with tales of bombing raids and struggle and hardship and loss (both my parents' extended families were decimated by war), rather than feel grateful that my own generation, by and large, avoided the fate that had overtaken our parents and grandparents – and of which we were continually reminded – we, some of us, felt our own escape to be a kind of curse. How was I to compete with my grandfather's ordeal as a private at Vimy Ridge? Or with my uncle, a hero of the battle of Monte Cassino? My own childhood was spent in the fake and sleazy Formica zone of the sixties, and by the time I had reached my late teens there were no risks to be taken other than the ones we contrived to set up for ourselves.

The story about Cochrane and the Spanish Republicans set me thinking for other reasons, also. It not only illustrated how one person's moment of inspiration can save the lives of others; but how a particular kind of intelligence, the kind that cannot be forced to follow rules or accept predictable conclusions, could improvise a solution, find a way through, which other, more conventional minds, would never have considered. Cochrane's life seems to have followed this pattern of refusing the obvious, challenging received wisdom, even if, at times, the solutions that he reached were successful, as it were, for the wrong reasons. He had a mastery of the serendipitous gesture, an instinct perhaps, and after the war he became known internationally as a leading figure in the treatment of pneumoconiosis, working with the miners of the south Wales valleys, who came to trust and respect him.

But to return to 1941: immediately following his capture on Crete, Cochrane was dispatched by his captors to run the medical team in a prisoner of war camp at Thessalonika, and after that, to various other camps, including, as the war progressed, to Elsterhorst, in Germany. There, as he writes in his autobiography, the Germans delivered a young Soviet prisoner to his ward late one night. What followed was to have a marked effect on both him and his understanding of the practice of medicine.

> The ward was full, so I put him in my room as he was moribund and screaming and I did not want to wake the ward. I examined him. He had obvious gross bilateral cavitation and a severe pleural rub. I thought the latter was the cause of the pain and the screaming. I had no morphia, just aspirin, which had no effect.
>
> I felt desperate. I knew very little Russian then and there was no one in the ward who did. I finally instinctively sat down on the bed and took him in my arms, and the screaming stopped almost at once. He died peacefully in my arms a few hours later. It was not the pleurisy that caused the screaming but loneliness. It was a wonderful education about the care of the dying. I was ashamed of my misdiagnosis and kept the story secret.

I envisage the scene as though it were from a black and white film, in fact I see the whole episode in monochrome. Cochrane speaks with the clipped accents of his caste, the physical image forming in my consciousness of a young Dirk Bogarde (though not in his ludicrous 'Doctor in the House' persona), despite the fact that I know what Cochrane looked like, from photographs of the period, and am struck by the startling evolution of his face and his manner, from the picture of the suave, pensively debonair undergraduate at Cambridge, puffing on his pipe; to the sternly bearded officer photographed in the uniform of the Spanish International Brigades in 1937; to the weary figure, dressed in British khaki, eyes fixed unblinkingly on the photographer – eyes which have by now absorbed unspeakable horrors, and which are at once resolute, knowing, gentle – taken at the end of the war.

The small room, which serves both as office and bedroom, lies at the end of the ward nearest the entrance through which the patient has been escorted by guards. The desk is cluttered with papers and empty cartons, the bed unmade. The doctor rarely sleeps for more than two or three hours at a time. Cochrane, concerned, humane, yet anxious that the screaming will distress others on his ward of suffering prisoners, is at a loss what to do. He thinks, with good reason, that the pain and screaming are caused by the condition of the Russian's mangled lungs. There are no effective drugs. His desperation is made worse by his lack of Russian, and the absence of any interlocutor, anyone to intercede, or in any way to communicate with the patient in a language he might understand, and in telling us this – "I knew very little Russian then" – Cochrane infers that he would not remain forever ignorant of that language (a keen linguist, he also spoke Spanish, after serving in an ambulance unit during the Civil War, where he saw action at the siege of Madrid and the battle of Jarama, as well as on the Aragon front; and he was fluent in Dutch and in German, having studied medicine in Leiden, and psychiatry in Vienna and Berlin before the war). A person who is linguistically gifted probably feels a greater frustration than the monoglot when confronted with a situation in which communication is hindered by lack of a common language, and communication, or its absence, is at the heart of this account of Cochrane's, as it appears to be in so much else about the man, otherwise why would he make a point of adding "and there was no one in the ward who did [speak Russian]". It was imperative for him to communicate something to this screaming patient, and language, the patient's own language, is the first and most obvious faculty in which Cochrane finds himself lacking, along with adequate painkillers. So, "instinctively", he takes the soldier in his arms. What else can he do? Where language has failed, this instinctive response to hold the man, to take him in his arms, to comfort him, yields immediate results. The screaming stops "almost at once".

Who is the Russian soldier? What is his story? In the cinematic version that unfolds before me as I read this account, I can barely perceive the extent of his suffering and his pain; we are allowed only this glimpse of him, dying in Cochrane's arms, his story is known only in its culmination, as though everything that came before were blacked out; Cochrane, like us, knows nothing of his past, he could be any peasant or worker drafted into the vast Soviet army ploughing westward across the steppes, pursuing their German invaders after the nightmares of Stalingrad and Kursk, it is of little account because shortly he will be dead, still lying in Cochrane's arms; we know nothing of his demons, of his dreams, of his sweetheart back in the ruins of a bombed-out city, of his mother picking through the rubble for coal and scraps of food – nothing of the life he led before the war, let alone the life he might have led had there been no war – we have only Cochrane's words, his certainty that "it was not the pleurisy that caused the screaming but loneliness" which is not to say that pleurisy is painless – it delivers a relentless, searing pain – but that the pain caused by the pleurisy was nowhere near as significant as the pain caused by loneliness: if not hyperbole, the statement that the soldier stops screaming almost immediately is an astonishing and moving testament to the humanity of Cochrane, holding this dying, then dead man in his arms, rocking him gently – the text suggests that he held the man for several hours – there in the squalid room leading off the ward filled with other no doubt appallingly wounded, sick and dying men. And if the word "wonderful" shocks us in the next sentence, coming so precipitately after the patient's death, we also learn that for Cochrane, the experience was an "education", but one, that, paradoxically, he claims to have concealed, being "ashamed" of his "misdiagnosis". And then, he tells us, he kept the story secret (on account of his shame) but clearly does not do so now, since by telling us, in his memoir, he is betraying his own secret. Of what then is he ashamed? Can it really be that he is ashamed of his misdiagnosis? *Is* there a misdiagnosis? The man has shattered lungs and is in pain: this much Cochrane diagnoses correctly. What he claims to be a misdiagnosis is what constitutes the source of the patient's pain (and screaming). It is hard to sanction his statement that he kept silent simply because he had attributed the patient's screaming to the pain he was suffering on account of his broken lungs.

There lies at the end of the story this obscure question mark, this reluctant admission to having guarded a secret over many years, which cannot simply be accounted for by the reason that Cochrane gives, of having made, in his words, a misdiagnosis. Could it be that this concealment, even this belatedly revealed form of concealment, conceals another, more obscure secret, one perhaps connected to his having held the Soviet prisoner in his arms, like a lover, for several hours? Do those words 'ashamed' and 'secret' reveal more than they were intended to?

I want, like Cochrane, to believe that the soldier died peacefully. Without that peaceful death the story would have no meaning. And I want to insist that it was his imagination, rather than simply his instinct, which allowed Cochrane to discover that the patient was screaming through fear and loneliness rather than because of the pain in his chest. It is Cochrane's imagination that steers the whole story, his ability to transcend the spectacular misery of the prison hospital, his offering to the patient a flake of humanity in the desolate confines of the enemy compound. It is a story, in short, that celebrates the redemptive powers of the imagination.

14

My attic study is full of books, around a thousand of them, of which I might have read a half, the others lie in wait; some were bought years ago and are destined to remain unread, others were consumed as soon as I brought them home. Some, more ancient acquisitions, glare back at me accusingly, claiming their right to be read, to be given the chance to relieve me of some particularly acute area of ignorance, of which I possess legion, there is never enough time to read all these books, there never will be time enough, there is never enough time in one life to read everything. Writing this, my gaze lingers on a section of shelving near the desk, where a number of city, regional and national guides are lined up: a collection that tells its own story, both of trips fulfilled and trips fantasised. In addition there are studies of, or first-hand accounts of those cities that I have lived in, or have visited more than once, or which hold a particular interest for me: New York, Tokyo, Buenos Aires and Barcelona.

Alongside the guidebooks, at the end of the shelf, lie a pile of notebooks, some filled with photographs of trips made to Japan and the Americas, and lying on top of these is a quietly ticking device: a notebook, given to me as a present by a friend, Annie, for my birthday in 2004. It is a small artist's sketch book, blue and green with a black seam, which, upon opening, reveals a brief birthday greeting, followed, on the next page, in thick black italic script, by the words, or title, Selected Permutations. The reader, thus introduced to the notion that this is to be a conceptual gift, will turn the page to find: 'If you take 7 items, they can be re-arranged in 5,040 ways.' Flicking the page, we are invited to extend our horizons: 'Add one more, making 8, and there are 40,320.' But this reference to the number eight is merely a digression, an illustration of the huge increase in permutations available in the arrangement of eight items rather than seven, and when we turn the page again it is revealed that the 'items' in question are in fact *words*, and that we are going to deal only with seven of them:

1. *One life is not enough for everything*, seven words which, together, in that order, represent Proposition Number One, the first in a long

run of variations or permutations, and the one we might take to be the key or default position, the argument, the starting place, the point at which we enter the infinite labyrinth of possibility, as Borges might have said.

The book does not contain 5,040 permutations of course (there are not enough pages) – only a selection of them, 57 to be exact, one for every thick page. Many of these permutations are fairly nonsensical, or at the very least, profoundly ungrammatical. The book's pages present us with a selection of cryptic utterances, for instance:

    39: One life, not for enough, is everything.
    1689: Is not one for life everything enough?
    2350: Not life enough. Everything is for one.

And finally, permutation 5040: *Everything for enough not is life one*, a simple inversion of the word order of Proposition Number One.

In a way, these permutations represent a snub to the notion of destiny, since, if we accept the idea of a single pre–determined outcome to our existence, then one life would, in fact, be enough for everything. Or to put it another way, one life would be enough to fulfil our specific destiny in that life, notwithstanding the possibility that we may have other lives. There are those too, for whom life presents no element of choice, or else very little. It is this predicament, of having no choice, from which I flee, from which perhaps we all flee. But that is not the point. The origin of this book of permutations lay in my conversations with this friend, Annie, about the impossibility of pursuing several options at once in certain life situations, even if those options do not at first seem mutually exclusive, of our having to abandon certain paths, of having to make choices between options (or permutations) even though we cannot know for sure whether those choices are the most propitious ones. Having decided that we can know only this life – even if there are others, of which we are unaware, in parallel or contiguous with this one – it is essential that we accept the limitations of this one life and turn those limitations to strategic advantage.

Unfortunately I do not know precisely how this is done. Perhaps that is the part we all struggle with, the fact that our lives are by their very nature limited. The premise is not contestable: one life *is* not enough for everything. Indeed, some lives are so brief that they barely register at all, they are scraps of flotsam on the tide of endless oblivion, or a faint bleeping on the bedside machinery, while others (like the Soviet soldier's) are so horribly curtailed as to make a nonsense of any notion of choice. When I start thinking in these terms, my own predicament does not seem quite so bad.

15

While trying to avoid writing one afternoon, I decide that I want to clear my desk, in fact to clear it and thoroughly clean it. I begin by brushing and then wiping the poorly varnished surface with an anti-bacterial cloth. It still looks dirty; ingrained gubbins of all varieties spread across the desktop. I reach into the low cupboard that extends beneath the eaves of this attic room, find sandpaper and apply myself to the task, scraping away with fixed determination. I begin thinking of the story I am supposed to be writing, of the book review I have promised to deliver, of the poems that lie unfinished in a drawer, but mostly I fall to thinking about the very act of writing, and how it consumes my life in so many ways, most of them satisfying in one sense or another; I like to write, I enjoy what my friend Niall Griffiths calls the glorious mix of exhaustion and exhilaration that come at the end of a good session, the almost trancelike state one enters when entirely absorbed in the life of a character or a place, of having captured some small truth and transcribed it successfully so that a total stranger, on reading it, can nod or laugh in recognition of something shared, or something learned, though possibly always known. But the downside, the part that most writers dread, is the seemingly interminable agony one enters when, for some reason or other, one is kept from writing, either by illness, other work, or a general reluctance to face the blank screen; or else besieged by the feeling that whatever one writes has been said before, and probably better, elsewhere, and yet the terrible arrogance of the author, the desire to act God, that insistent striving to give voice, will not subside.

In this condition, I find myself considering the plight of Bartleby, as described by Enrique Vila-Matas in his book of that name. Bartleby is the type of those who are conditioned to write, for whom writing is default behaviour, and yet who, when asked to perform a particular job or favour, will answer, as a matter of principle, *I'd rather not*, regardless of the question, and who, in similar vein, will courageously decline to write at all, although deemed to be a 'writer' in the eyes of the world. Vila-Matas has researched the type well:

For some time now I have been investigating the frequent examples of Bartleby's syndrome in literature, for some time I have studied the illness, the disease endemic to contemporary letters, the negative impulse or attraction towards nothingness that means that certain creators, while possessing a very demanding literary conscience (or perhaps precisely because of this), never manage to write: either they write one or two books and then stop altogether or, working on a project, seemingly without problems, one day they become paralysed for good.

Vila-Matas does not regard the state of being a Bartleby to be quite beyond hope. There is a glimmer on the horizon, and he contrives, in some way, to conjure an (as yet) invisible text out of the footnotes he has prepared for it. "I wonder if I can do this," he writes. "I am convinced that only by tracking down the labyrinth of the No can the paths still open to the writing of the future appear. I wonder if I can evoke them." He occupies himself, over the course of the book, by investigating these writers of the No, giving cameo performances to writers with an overdeveloped sense of the absurdity of their vocation, or with an extraordinary capacity for prevarication and delay.

The list of writers that Vila-Matas compiles of Bartlebys past and present is extensive and includes such luminaries as Rimbaud, Walser, Gil de Biedma and Salinger, even Beckett. There is a peculiar sense in which these writers turn the act of not-writing into a virtue, of which it is hard not to be envious. One of the most outstanding examples is Joseph Joubert, a Frenchman who lived in the eighteenth century and who "discovered a delightful place where he could digress and end up not writing a book at all." Although he lived to be seventy, Joubert "never wrote a book. He only prepared himself to write one, single-mindedly searching for the right conditions. Then he forgot this purpose as well." Ah, the nefarious comforts of silence! Some of Vila-Matas' writers of the No, such as Robert Walser, the shy and reclusive author of *The Walk*, turn not-writing itself into a topic of their oeuvre (Walser spent the last twenty years of his life as the inmate of an asylum for the insane, as such institutions were then known). The dedication with which Walser and others pursued their calling raises the frightening possibility that I am not yet good enough, or sufficiently dedicated, to be a Bartleby; that despite my good intentions, to fail so self-consciously, and in so spectacular a way as to provoke the admiration of other, more orthodox writers (those who put pen to paper) is an achievement beyond my skills and powers of endurance.

By now I am scrubbing so hard that most of the surface is spotless; the dirty varnish is gone and I am sanding raw wood. The desk is a large one; I have covered a big area and am still going strong. The thought occurs to me that if I just keep on sandpapering that desk, it will eventually cease to exist. I could entirely transform my room (the desk, as I have said, is substantial) and in the process, as I scrape away in this alchemical act of molecular disassembly – of making something disappear, of making nothing out of something – I could consider the book I am writing, measuring it out in my mind, scene by scene, chapter by chapter, so that by the time I have rasped away the last grains of sawdust from the last chip of wood, I will be ready to continue. True, I would no longer have a desk to write it on, I would have to sit in the armchair and use a notebook or the laptop, but that would surely be a small loss compared with the relief of knowing the outcome of my story. And at least I have the laptop, which is just as well, seeing as my handwriting has become quite illegible, I can hardly make it out, and even when I concentrate and force myself to write very slowly the result resembles nothing but a spider-trail of flattened hieroglyphs. My typing isn't up to much either, but at least I can read what I have written and stand a much better chance of guessing my own intentions, despite all the typos and unintentional neologisms that occupy the screen, underlined in green and red. It is frustrating, but I have to put up with this disability, just as I endure the laborious task of reading; for even though reading remains a pleasure, it is one that stretches my powers of concentration to the limit. Recently it took me three weeks to read a short novel, simply because I had to re-read every paragraph several times in order to retain the gist of whatever was going on, and neither was it a particularly demanding book; the same thing happens whether I am reading philosophy or a detective novel. This is hard for me, since I have always had good powers of retention, and it feels strange and disempowering to be struggling through the page like a seven-year-old, and remembering not a thing.

16

I receive an email from a Canadian friend, the poet and DJ Kerry-Lee Powell. In it, she tells how she recently passed a homeless woman on a park bench in Ottawa, who had lined up beside her some books for sale, one of which was a collection of my poems. Kerry-Lee writes that this event was noteworthy – apart from the remarkable odds against anyone in Ottawa actually owning a book of my poetry – because only the night before I had, she said, figured in a dinner party conversation about Byron Foster, who was murdered by bandits in Belize in 1996. Byron was a friend of mine from the London years. We met at university, and although we lost touch for most of the eighties (when I lost touch with almost everyone) we had begun to exchange letters two years before his death. I have a letter in front of me, dated 24th September, 1994. He talks of homesteading in the jungle. "Bar a couple of rum sessions, I've been stone cold sober for three months. At this moment I'm on my own on a moonless night with the Milky Way straddling the sky, in an open-walled thatched shed in a large stretch of rain forest. There are tadpoles in a puddle in the tire marks, howler monkeys, armadillos, toucans, even a puma based a mile or so away. We haven't met as yet. I have a 16 gauge. There is no electricity. I'm blessed with wife and kids. Though I've worked 6 years for this, I feel too lucky." He doesn't mention the desperados, the outlaws, men who live in the jungle, though he must have been aware of them. The six years he refers to is the time he has spent saving for his little garden of eternity, where he plans to watch his children grow. While he prepares the land and works on the house, he has sent his family back to Belize City, until it is time for them to join him.

Then, one night they come for him, the men from the jungle. When his wife's family turn up at the homestead, not having heard from Byron for too long, they find his body, but not his gun.

And those specific events, the ones leading to Byron's death, I had only discovered during a phone conversation with David Lan, another friend from the London School of Economics. I asked him, in the course of our chat, what news he had of Byron, to which he replied with a long silence, before proceeding to tell me the outline of the story, filling out the details when we met a few days later in the café of the Young Vic theatre in London, where David works as artistic director.

Byron was one of the first friends I made at the LSE, although he was older than me and in his final year. He had the manner of an East End wide boy, and had some serious drugs charges on his record before he ever came to be a student, in fact I believe it was only the promise of a place at university that kept him from being sent down for a substantial spell. He had been through rehab as well, at least once, and these things set him apart from the usual run of students. Eventually, Byron acquired a first class honours degree, then went on to Cambridge and studied for a PhD. He travelled to Belize to do his fieldwork among the Garifuna people and, like other anthropologists before him, stayed on, put off by every visit to Thatcher's England, until he realised that the idea of return was entirely impossible. Besides, he had by now acquired a wife and children, as he mentions in his letter just before the portentous words 'I feel too lucky'.

Byron's comment on his recent abstinence from alcohol was most likely a direct response to my own, which I must have mentioned in a letter to him, as I had myself given up drinking. When we were close friends, however, in the late 1970s, our activities involved long nights of inebriation around the metropolis, and the consumption of a wide range of stimulants and narcotics; and because of Byron's network of underworld associates, I came into contact with some of the most sinister people I have ever met.

Byron moved in a way that resembled the passage of someone forever on a mission that required swift resolution, so much so that his walk, even his manner of crossing a room, became a kind of allegory of his mental manoeuvring; he was always hunting, always on the lookout, though evidently not with sufficient guile to save his own life.

I spent those years in London at a variety of addresses: Finsbury Park, Leytonstone, Walthamstow and Hackney. I was swept up on the tide of punk, attended lots of concerts, including early gigs by the Sex

Pistols at the 100 Club, and the Clash's famous Rainbow event when most of the seating was destroyed by enthusiastic fans. I wrote a lot of bad poems, or rants, all fortunately lost, and later even got to read at various gigs, notably performing an impromptu session at a Cure concert at the North-East London Polytechnic in Walthamstow, around the time of their first hit, *Killing an Arab*. I toyed with the idea of a band, like so many others, but we never got more than a couple of shambolic performances. Unlike Joe Strummer, I felt too self-consciously middle class to be a real punk; besides, it seemed an insurmountable obstacle, belonging to something whose essence lay in not belonging to anything, and which had, by the late seventies, already been colonized by the very forces of exploitative capitalism that it set out to destroy.

Nor did I find what I was looking for in anthropology and decided, rather prematurely, that I was not suited to an academic career, although there were many aspects of the subject that fascinated me. I was highly critical of the methodologies on offer and more than a little sceptical: specifically I took issue with what I considered to be a neo-colonialist cultural voyeurism at the heart of the discipline – it was no coincidence that the study of anthropology originated in the British and French imperial past – and the assumption that anthropologists had some kind of edict or warrant to analyse and evaluate cultures other than their own. The discipline of anthropology seemed to confirm the utter evisceration of the cultures under examination, and as such constituted the ultimate exploitation. One thing I took from the experience however, was that for over two million years we have been a species of hunters and gatherers, and the settlements and cities of the past few thousand years are a mere blip in that continuum. We are nomads and hunter-gatherers who have forgotten ourselves: but at some profound level we are still out there hunting and foraging, hauling fragments of booty back to our imaginary caves.

In spite of a muted respect for intellectual achievement, I forsook the lectures of Karl Popper and left after two years of study, or rather, I never returned for the third year, having got involved in an impassioned and tortuous affair with a woman to whom I was later married, then separated, though remaining friends (a rather optimistic term considering the flammability of the relationship) and occasionally lovers, until her death in 1988.

When we met in 1977, Natasha, who had grown up in Australia, was twenty-three, and had recently moved into an empty house, two doors down from our place in Leytonstone, along with her friend Sadie. The two women were rumoured to be lovers. I was invited to their squat for a party – a neighbourly gesture – but did not catch sight of Natasha until, wandering through the house at seven in the morning, when most of the guests had either left or fallen asleep, I saw this dark, feline girl, apparently naked beneath a carelessly draped blanket, slinking down the stairs, a bottle of red wine in one hand, a half-smoked joint in the other. This dishevelled vision, with its suggestion of one practised in debauchery, impressed me deeply. The second time I visited Natasha and Sadie's house was after an evening with the two of them at the Three Blackbirds in Leyton High Street and I fell asleep on their sofa. When I awoke my jeans had been cut to threads, and Natasha was curled up next to me on the sofa, leafing through a magazine. She excelled at sending mixed messages of a complex kind, and this intrigued me at first, although it later drove me to distraction.

Over that summer I worked on a building site in Leytonstone and in the autumn the three of us travelled to Italy and stayed with Natasha's aunt and uncle in Florence. In November we moved on to Crete, where we spent much of the winter, joining the migrant workforce on the island.

In the spring of 1978 Natasha and I were back in east London, where we rented a nice house in St Marks' Rise, Dalston, just up from Ridley Road market. I began work as a sawyer in one of the many reproduction furniture factories in that part of town and Natasha started work for a music publisher in Shoreditch. We did a lot of drugs, but such habits are costly, and after falling behind with the rent, we moved to a squat near Newington Green, where I started in a different factory, also in Shoreditch. The work was undemanding and I was given a job at a higher hourly rate. I decided that we should clean up our act and start saving, in order to put a deposit on a flat. Then, one morning, sober and alert, I chopped two fingers off my left hand while operating a ripsaw. There had been a sudden breach in the density of the wood I was pushing through the saw, and my hand slipped forward onto the blade: in the industrial inquiry that followed it was revealed that the safety guard had been modified to make the saw more productive. At first I did not realise what had happened, although I stopped working, stepped back from the workbench, and was determinedly not looking at my left hand. Then I saw one of the fork-lift truck drivers – who had stopped his machine and was staring at me, horrified – turn aside and throw up, and I knew that something was badly wrong. A Jamaican workmate hurried over, and lifted my arm, telling me I must keep it elevated. An ambulance arrived, and I was taken to a hospital in Bethnal Green, where the nurse looking after me burst into tears on seeing my hand, which did nothing to reassure me – I still did not want to look – but she at least allowed me a cigarette, despite the no-smoking signs that furnished the walls of the emergency room.

I was taken to a specialist hospital in Billericay, with my left index finger in an ice pack on the seat beside me, and there surgeons attempted to re-attach the missing digit, but these were the early days of micro-surgery, and the finger did not take. During my stay in hospital Natasha visited me every day and we drank brandy in the conservatory that was attached to my ward, overlooking a lawn and pretty, well-tended gardens. I wrote a lot of poetry, and was visited by some of the East End miscreants I had befriended through Byron, who insisted, in spite of my protestations, on rolling me a succession of spliffs, and one day on the lawn outside the ward Natasha asked me if I would marry her, although I thought it probably wasn't a good idea, we really weren't very good for each other, and I suspected that her proposal came out of sympathy for my recent maiming. We got married anyway.

After hospitalisation and recovery, I found a job as a milkman with Unigate Dairies, and over the bleak and freezing winter of 1978-9 was allocated a round that covered Highbury and Finsbury Park. The early starts meant that I could finish by midday and spend the remainder of the afternoon at our local Irish pub. This was the era of IRA bombings and English antipathy towards the Irish at large. Big Tom, the landlord, had Republican sympathies and there were often scenes of extraordinary intemperance, all-night lock-ins and impromptu police raids, of which we always seemed to receive advance warning, and were herded down into the cellar, sometimes for hours at a time. I still have nightmarish visions of driving through the snow and ice at five in the morning after a night at Tom's, tripping on acid, and wrestling the steering wheel from Natasha, who, not untypically, had attempted to steal the milk float. Natasha got into fights with women who spoke to me too freely, but was promiscuous herself when drinking, pushed against people in the street, and sometimes danced like a dervish through the traffic, particularly when angry. She was a sensuous, wilful drunk, passionate, provocative and unpredictable.

After three months as a milkman, I was walking home with Natasha from breakfast at a local café when I was leapt upon by two plain clothes detectives, bundled into a squad car, and transported at great speed, with siren blaring, to Dalston Police Station, where I was locked in a padded cell, mattresses stacked ominously against the walls – a clear indication that my captors intended to secure a full confession. My arresting officer, Detective Sergeant F, referred to me as a milkman *of ill repute*, and insisted that he was going to *send me down*. I expected at least a good kicking, which, after all, was standard Met procedure in the 1970s. But Natasha had managed to get hold of a lawyer, who turned up just in time to get me released on the grounds of *habeas corpus*.

My account books were not in order, and I was accused of theft, or rather, not charging customers for their deliveries, which amounted to the same thing. After three hearings before a magistrate, the case eventually went to crown court, where I faced trial for theft and defrauding my employers, a significant crime under British law. I was, however, fortunate enough to be defended by a young barrister called Helena Kennedy and, after a week-long trial, all charges against me were thrown out. The local newspaper called me the Robin Hood of the Dairies, a rather flattering appellation.

Considering the volatility of our relationship – not to mention the reputation we acquired among our friends – and the extreme behaviour that we seemed to encourage in each other, it was amazing that either Natasha or I survived into the eighties, but for a few months into the new decade things actually calmed down, and we led a relatively sedate domestic life. When Natasha became pregnant I bought a suit and found work selling advertising for employers in the emerging computing industry. I went to work each day in an office in Chancery Lane. My income rocketed, but Natasha had a miscarriage at six months, and the money we had saved was rapidly discharged on the purchase of a better class of drugs and long evenings in Soho bars. Soho had been the haunt of Natasha's beautiful and bohemian mother, Francesca, during the late 1940s, where she had befriended the likes of Dylan Thomas, Francis Bacon, Lucien Freud, and the two Bernard brothers – Bruce and Jeffrey, the subject of the Keith Waterhouse play *Jeffrey Bernard is Unwell*. I got to know Bruce, the photographer, quite well. On one occasion we walked into The French House, our preferred Soho hostelry, and were met by an astonished greeting, as a sozzled and prematurely aged Lothario tottered over, arms outstretched, in the belief that Natasha was Francesca, and that he had wandered into a felicitous thirty-year time warp.

Although it had probably not been a good idea for us to have considered having a child at all, we were both badly affected by our loss. The relationship began gradually to deteriorate, and we spent long spells not speaking to each other, which wasn't easy, since we lived in a small terraced house in Walthamstow. We started to go our separate ways. I continued for a while in selling and advertising, jobs I hated and from which my earnings never lasted; all of them involved me talking bullshit for money and all of them, I knew, would poison my soul for as long as I stayed in them. In the summer I took time off work to visit Spain on my own, travelling through Catalunya and across to Pamplona for the fiesta of San Fermín. In the autumn, I threw in my last job in advertising newspaper space in order to drift around south-west France on my own for a month, finding work on the grape harvest, which I regarded as a kind of ritual obeisance to the god Dionysus.

By this time, I had developed a serious problem with alcohol. If I started to drink, whatever my intentions, I would usually continue until I was incoherent and unconscious, and this had been going on for years, since my teens. Cutting down was never really the issue with me: I knew that I had to stop, that it was all or nothing. But the truth was, at this time, and for years to come, I could not conceive of a future that did not include alcohol. Every fantasy, every dream of happiness, every projection of future bliss, included booze in the equation. Every vision of erotic love was drenched in the stuff, *a jug of wine and thou*, and for fifteen years I drank to excess on every conceivable occasion. Sure, there were periods of abstinence, enforced by illness, hospitalisation, or the occasional stay in the cells, even, over the years, the odd, determined spell of self-imposed sobriety, though, apart from a period in Spain in 1988-9, these rarely lasted long enough to make any difference to the general trend, and are best viewed as aberrations in the otherwise consistently downward trajectory of my life, my one and only life, which is not enough for everything.

I tried, unsuccessfully, to sort myself out at a rehab day centre in Fulham, but was not ready for it, and besides, it was never going to be easy to stop while Natasha, who drank as much as I did, continued. Once, when I was laid low with glandular fever, a doctor carried out liver function tests, and told me that I was unlikely to live to the age of thirty if I continued the way I was heading.

In November, having received an advance payment on my industrial injuries claim, I made a trip to Ireland with Natasha, which brought our marriage, such as it was, to an end. Knowing that a separation was inevitable, I took a late-night flight from Dublin to London and found myself in the departures lounge at Heathrow with a wad of money in my pocket and no destination in mind, other than the desire to be somewhere warmer and drier than Dublin in November. I got into conversation with a group of Nigerians who were waiting for their flight to Lagos. Come to Nigeria, they said, you will like it there. I pondered this, while they expounded on the virtues of their homeland. We were overheard by a group of Kenyans, seated nearby, who joined the debate. Where should I go? Why, Kenya, of course. There is nowhere else like it in the whole of Africa. I would be a fool to go to Nigeria; the very thought of it! I left the two groups to continue their argument without me, and bought a ticket for the first destination on the continent of Africa, which happened to be Tunis. It wouldn't be as warm as Nairobi, for sure, but was a lot cheaper to get to.

I arrived in Tunis, unaware, until I was actually there, of the mounting threat of war in that country. Colonel Gaddafi of Libya, who was already at war with Chad, had massed troops along the Tunisian border, following some territorial dispute with his neighbour. Security in the airport was high. As I passed through a customs hall thronging with armed police, the official asked me, perplexingly, "What is your function?" *My function?* My brain, addled by a week's uninterrupted whiskey-drinking in Dublin and a sleepless night at Heathrow, failed to come up with anything remotely sensible in English, let alone French. "I'm a writer," I said, floundering. "A journalist?" asked the official, his lips curling into what might have been a smile, but which to me indicated only the most profound suspicion. "No, just a poet," I added, realising, as I said it, that I was not doing myself any favours with this declaration. The customs officer seemed amused, then looked at me with a serious expression. "You are a writer? Please, *write* something!" He pushed a scrap of paper and a pen towards me, across the surface of the desk. I leaned over and wrote a couple of lines, the first thing that came into my head. The officer scrutinized what I had written. "Sign it," he ordered. I complied, adding a little flourish to my signature. He beamed at me, a happy man. "Thank you," he said, folding the piece of paper inside his breast pocket: "Welcome to Tunisia."

I took a taxi to a luxury hotel, bought a bottle of cognac, and retired to my room, drank the brandy, and slept for twenty-four hours. On waking, I showered, had some breakfast, and went to look for somewhere less expensive to stay. I found a place that had not seen a coat of paint since it was erected at the end of the nineteenth century, and a room where cockroaches infested the broken bidet and rats could be heard scuttling beneath the floorboards. I felt at home. I had no luggage, and needed a change of clothes. There was a market nearby. I bought a white linen suit, off the peg, which made me feel like a colonial official, and a couple of shirts.

That evening, I visited a tea-house on the edge of the medina, and sat outside under some trees, as a huge, orange moon crept above the rooftops to the west. I was joined by a young Tunisian, like me in his early twenties, and a couple of his friends, and we fell into conversation. They were students, and they spoke French. I was enjoying the cool open space, the dappled light of the trees under the streetlamps, the learning of names. However, we had not been talking for long when three military trucks pulled up at the roadside, and soldiers piled out, cordoning off the terrace where we were sitting. Around fifty of us were rounded up into groups of four or five, and an officer moved between the soldiers, giving orders. When he came to my group, my new friends told him I was a foreigner. The officer indicated that this information was of no interest to him, and that I was to be taken away, along with the others. I surmised that, in his eyes, strangers are no less likely to be spies. One of the boys I had been talking to persisted in his protest, and a younger officer muttered something to his chief. They asked me for papers, which I gave them. The older officer inspected my passport reluctantly, returned it. He told me I needn't come with them. The soldiers bundled fifty men into the back of the three trucks. One of the boys from my table turned and shrugged in my direction as they led him away. I sat alone outside the café for a while. The leaves rustled under the streetlamps. I didn't finish my tea. Rising from the table, I ventured inside. The café-owner was chatting with a cop and another man. When I offered to pay, the owner took the money without looking at me.

I headed down to Hammamet and stayed at a tourist hotel for a few nights, in a place that had pretensions towards the grand style, modelled on a Sultan's palace from the Thousand and One Nights, with vast dining halls, a ballroom and expansive gardens which led down to the sea. The place must have been hell in summer, but was almost tolerable in November. I had my meals brought up, drank a lot of brandy, wrote in my journal, and sweated the nights away in a delirium of dread and panic, which, however, did not stop me drinking. I missed Natasha with what felt like physical pain. I set off for the south of the country, where, I reckoned, at least there was desert.

After several days wandering around the south, and discovering that I had no desire to go on a camel trek with the few tourists that were about, I ended up lodging in a small town at the desert's edge, spending the daylight hours on the shaded patio of a tea-house, and sleeping in what appeared to be the owner's spare room. I wrote miserable monologues in my journal and read the *Tain*, the only book I had

69

with me, in Kinsella's translation, picked up in a Dublin bookstore. It was strange following the adventures of the mighty Cuchulain and other wild Irish heroes while holed up in a ramshackle tea-house on the edge of the Sahara.

Eventually, having read the *Tain* twice, I realised that I was wasting my time, and should return to London. I caught a boat from Tunis to Marseilles, the train to Paris, and the overnight boat train from the Gare du Nord to Waterloo. I arrived back in Walthamstow at around nine in the morning, let myself in and sat in the kitchen, staring at my supply of duty-free booze. I knew that I was not well, that I was undergoing some kind of emotional breakdown. My efforts to address my alcoholism at the clinic in Fulham had come to nothing, the therapy sessions only depressed me further (hearing other people's sorrowful stories did nothing but exacerbate my own misery). My thinking was displaced, or rather I felt alienated from myself, as if I had no control over the delirious onrush of unconnected thoughts and impulses that tossed me through the days and nights in a chaotic frenzy of drinking, and I had become increasingly erratic in my behaviour. For a while, Natasha and I had talked about going to live in Wales, and to this end we looked for a house in the Dolgellau area, even made an offer on a remote farmhouse in the shadow of Cader Idris, but this fell through after the trip to Dublin, and the idea of making plans together seemed quite pointless to me. I decided to get out. I moved in with friends in Clapton, and after a month of useless prevarication, I set out, catching the Dover-Calais ferry, on what was to be nine years of aimless, if philosophically enriching travel.

With the money I had at my disposal (after giving a third of it to Natasha I still had a substantial sum) I did not, at first, need to think about looking for work. I had an open invitation to stay in Florence with Natasha's Italian cousins (her aunt, Viola, had always been kind to me, and I got on well with her husband Michele, a poet and university professor). I stayed in Florence for a couple of months at the Villa Ranchetti, and then in April 1981 I headed back to Crete. I was harbouring a vague notion of travelling on to Alexandria, sailing down the Nile to Aswan, and from there continuing south into Sudan, cutting east into Kenya and down to Tanzania. That was the general plan, at any rate. But whether out of indolence, or as I preferred to think of it, principle – by which I avowed a dislike of Third World tourism, and was consequently not tempted to follow the hippy trail to India – I never made it down to Africa. In fact, apart from a couple of trips to Turkey, it was a long time before I ventured any further than Crete.

17

When I try to revisit, in my memory – in what counts for memory – that shadowy recess that claims knowledge of any one of those moments which have slipped beyond easy recall, I cannot help but conjure, alongside the actual sequence of events, a plethora of alternative outcomes, of the things that might have happened next but didn't, the numerous possible developments that could have been subsequent to each isolate action, the taking of another turning along the almost endless roads of my frequently aimless or random travels, the decision to stay another night, another day, for yet another drink, for the rain to pass; or as once occurred, and this I can recall quite distinctly, one penniless and leaden afternoon while walking some interminable road in Sicily and composing in my head a new rendition of *Stuck Inside of Mobile with the Memphis Blues Again,* turning the verses round and round with a melody that I remember still, singing aloud and walking with obtuse abandon across the barren centre of the island towards Palermo, for reasons which, however, I forget, a van pulled up and I climbed in and the two men, driver and passenger, brothers no doubt, or cousins, one of them, the passenger, with boils on his neck, half covered by the collar of his jacket, asked me if I was available for work, and if so, was I interested in employment as a shepherd, a guardian of sheep, looking after their family's flock? There was about them something persuasively medieval and I thought about this unusual request for a while as the landscape accelerated past me in a way that suggested quite another country to the one through which I had until then been walking at an idle pace (walking always presents a landscape as a constant, a necessary interlocutor, or adjunct, to the interminable dialogue of the self) and told them in my rickety but ambitious Italian, in which I attempted to compensate by improvisation for what I lacked in vocabulary, that I didn't think the pastoral life was right for me, that I was heading for the city where friends awaited me (a fabrication, but also a potential truth, we never know from which asylum or harbour-front bar our friends are going to emerge). Not that I distrusted them entirely, but the proposal seemed so entirely preposterous that I was enchanted by it; such things happen far too often when engaged in a life of aimless wandering and only serve to show how tenuous are the routes we take, how already at the moment of their asking I was imagining the rocky hillside and the pastures upon which I would stroll as the sheep grazed peacefully and a large dog of indeterminate race and friendly disposition bounded at my side, and the simple shack or cottage to which I would retire at nightfall close by a tumbling brook, and where, of an evening I would drink my soup and eat my beans and spicy sausage, and record the modest happenings of the day in a tattered notebook, and as soon as I had dismissed this conjecture, and had rejected their offer, in that moment, in which the Arcadian fantasy had momentarily been conjured and abandoned, a choice was made, an option (albeit one which, in all probability, would have had an utterly tedious, farcical, or even tragic conclusion) was wiped from the slate, consigned to the void of things that did not happen, nor ever would. And so why is it that these possible solutions, these outcomes that, however improbable, might have come to pass, hold such a sway over my memory, even now, many years after the event, and, multiplied by several thousand such moments when a dice was thrown, a card called, an offer − *Will you come with me to Santorini?* − accepted or turned down, continue to plant in me a shadow of the life not lived? And this I need to get quite straight, this I need to emphasise with all the means at my disposal, which are the words I write: the experience is not one of sadness or regret for a path not taken, but a fluttering excitement, a fleeting, evanescent thrill at the thorough randomness of all existence, of the multitude of choices laid before me every day that I lived as a wanderer and a vagrant, at times igniting in me an almost religious zeal at not being beholden to anyone or anything, the purest fusion of detachment and of participation, that perpetual paradox, to be there and yet to be elsewhere, to be one and yet to be the other, because wherever I travelled I sensed that, however dire the circumstances, once you have learned to trust in the imagination, anything and everything seems possible.

However, it was brought to my attention on more than one occasion that imagination, when applied by the enforcers of law and order, could manifest itself in most perverse and punitive ways. A month or so before the episode I have just described, I was sleeping rough outside Messina, in the company of a friend from Crete, a young Englishman called Stuart, like myself an international vagabond. Stuart was an athletic type, with blonde curly hair and a strange propensity for falling in love with women who suffered from some minor physical blemish or disfigurement; a twisted lip or a pronounced limp would precipitate him into a state of uncontained erotic anticipation. Apart from this peculiar fetish, and a passion for fishing, he had few interests, but was a congenial companion nonetheless. I worked with him on the orange harvest in Crete, picking melons and grapes on Zakinthos, and on construction work in Sicily. While he worked, Stuart would often sing, quite badly, a common trait among building labourers; we are all familiar with those tuneless outbursts, which drift on the malignant city air from the upper rungs of scaffolding on hot afternoons. His favourite song went like this:

> I remember the night
> I fell in the shite
> I had my best suit on

The song ended there, however, since Stuart could not remember the rest of the words, if indeed there were any. He also sang a song, in an affected upper-class accent, composed by a well-known English eccentric that went as follows:

> As I walk along the pier
> With an independent air
> I can hear the girls declare
> He must be a millionaire!

Both of these musical extracts, as sung by Stuart, ended on an up-tone, as though looking to the future with brave intent. I grew to detest his singing, but was able to forgive him, given his genial good nature, along with a residual sense of guilt for having lost his dog, Aris, a skinny and amiable mongrel, after being entrusted with its care in the city of Patras. The last news I heard of Stuart he had settled on Zakinthos, where he was working for a fisherman. Stuart dreamed of owning his own fishing launch and marrying one of the fisherman's seven daughters (I assume there was one with a suitable deformity). I have no idea whether he ever accomplished either of these ambitions.

We had travelled down the length of Italy together, heading for the peace camp at Comiso, an Italian version of Greenham Common, where protesters attempted, fruitlessly (or successfully, seen in a positive light, and in the subsequent curtailment of the Cold War) to stall and obstruct the deployment of cruise missiles by the American Air Force on the adjoining base. Stuart's last job, in Hania, had been as gardener at the villa of Constantinos Mitsodakis (who would shortly become prime minister of Greece) and consequently he travelled with some basic gardening tools in a sports bag, relics of his last employment, as he hoped to find similar work elsewhere, even, who knows, lend a hand to the peace activists by planting beans and carrots, a conjecture which I have no means of verifying now, having last seen Stuart one September day in the port of Githion in 1986. We had some kind of argument, I forget the details, but a lot of alcohol was involved, and that night I unwittingly boarded a ship bound for Alexandria, where I slept beneath a life-boat, waking, in a state of considerable disarray, many hours later, to the surprise of two Egyptian sailors, who were kind enough to accompany me to visit their skipper, one Captain Vassilikos. However.

On this earlier occasion, we had spent the night in a local bar and were settling down for a night's sleep on some wasteland at the city's edge, when, without warning, we were surrounded by gun-toting Carabinieri, who shone flashlights in our faces and demanded that we get up and come with them.

Italy was undergoing a perennial spell of political upheaval; the Red Brigades were at the pinnacle of their fame, and draconian legislation had been introduced, allowing the police to hold suspects for long periods without a trial. After being put up overnight in a police cell, we were interviewed separately the following morning. Stuart, who spoke no Italian, went first. Within minutes, an officer was sent to retrieve me, as the interrogation had come unstuck with the first question, namely, whether or not Stuart required a lawyer, a mere formality, though one which, in many countries, police officers are required to pose. Stuart was struggling under the misapprehension that he was being offered a tropical fruit for breakfast, since the Italian for lawyer, *avvocato*, closely resembles the word for the central ingredient of guacamole. I explained the misunderstanding to the astonished captain of Carabinieri, who, along with his colleagues, several of whom were crowded into the office, on finally grasping the cause of Stuart's parallel stupefaction, fell about laughing. Their mirth, however, did not save us from immediate incarceration. Since we had no money, we got no lawyer. So it was that Stuart and I were cast into Messina jail, ostensibly for being suspicious characters, and, to add a farcical touch worthy of Ionesco, for possession of offensive weapons (Stuart's shears and secateurs). We spent a week in solitary confinement (though in adjoining cells) being fed on a diet of hard-boiled eggs, which were presented at random intervals through the security hatch, along with the occasional bowl of dubious and insipid vermicelli soup. The view from my little hatch was depressing: I could see only the row of cell doors arranged along the facing corridor, and on the first day, for at least an hour, terrible sounds emanated from the one directly opposite my own, bloodcurdling oaths, which naturally provoked the thought that one of my fellow prisoners was being subjected to acts of torture. Peering out, I saw the victim, twitching and shaking in spasmodic hysteria, dragged from his cell by a guard and a trustee prisoner, and the latter pouring the contents of a bottle of red wine down the inmate's throat. I guessed he had been suffering from a bad dose of delirium tremens. In any case he immediately calmed down and was returned, silent now, to his cell.

On the first day as new inmates we were visited, an apparently routine affair, by the prison governor. He demanded to know if I was comfortably installed, a ridiculous proposition given the circumstances of my detention, and whether I had any particular requirements that he could fulfil. I asked for pen and paper and inquired whether there was a prison library from which I could borrow books, to help me fill out the unforeseeable number of days ahead. He nodded, acceding to my modest request, and said that these things would be attended to. Several hours passed, and after a while I imagined the governor's ready acceptance to be a bluff, designed to humiliate me, when a trustee prisoner knocked on my hatch, and passed me a prolific selection of pornographic magazines. These were to be my only reading matter for the duration of my stay, other than the desperate and obscene scratchings on the wall beside my bunk. Among the magazines were a quantity of the crudest pictorial narratives imaginable, and my vocabulary of lewd Italian terms and pet names for private zones of the human anatomy and demands for the satisfaction of a range of bedroom activities expanded rapidly with the first half dozen stories, but then remained sadly static, as the plot lines and the language followed a simple formula with few variations, much like any literature, but more so, and I reached what language teachers refer to as the intermediate plateau, where the command of lexis and syntax grinds to a halt, just as the same weary acts of bondage and subjugation, gropings, suckings, fuckings and floggings started to become as repetitive and predictable as, years before, had been the Three Bears' discovery of Goldilocks asleep in Baby Bear's bed.

Each morning we were given an exercise hour in a yard enclosed by high walls, where we mingled with other prisoners, and messages were passed, deals done, looks exchanged, insults delivered and returned, romances nurtured, enmities engendered or further advanced, alliances forged, resentments aired, the usual appalling range of activities either contemplated or acted upon, which take place, openly or in secret, with good will or malice, with intent to immediate profit or ulterior motive, whenever large groups of men are kept in confinement against their will, and where I met, or rather was befriended by, for reasons which would shortly become apparent, a young Italian-American, Marco, who was awaiting trial on a drugs charge, one which promised to curtail his freedom for many years to come. He had been living, so he said, on one of the Aeolian islands, which lie to the north of Sicily, and which are sparsely populated and known mainly for the farming of olives, and, a decade later, as being the location for the film *Il Postino*, starring Massimo Troisi as the eponymous postman and Philippe Noiret as the poet Pablo Neruda (in fact, Neruda's Italian exile was spent on the island of Capri, which, however, was far too despoiled by tourism to replicate the 1952 setting). Marco told me that his island home had been raided by police and he had been led, chained and manacled, through the village to the waiting police launch which was to bring him to Messina. I wondered if he was a very minor drug-dealer with bad luck and worse connections, or a big fish, some kind of Mafioso, to warrant such extreme and dramatic capture, it was difficult to tell, but he seemed happy to have found someone he could speak English with (his own variety was straight out of *Goodfellas*) and someone, moreover, from what I told him of our arrest and lack of criminal conviction (or even formal charge) who would, in all probability, shortly be released. He assured me that Stuart and I would not be held for long, once our records had been checked with Interpol and other agencies (I gulped at this, knowing that I was, completely innocently, and due to an execrable cock-up by the Greek police a year before, registered with Interpol) and mentioned that he might have a favour to ask me before I left.

On my way back to the cells, I passed a guard standing beside the metal gates at the entrance to the stairway of the block; he told me to wait a minute, delved in a bag, and handed me a fresh salami *imbottito*. After days of hard-boiled eggs and water, this was a feast. I thanked the guard, experiencing a spurt of hope for the future of humanity, broke the sandwich in half, and shared it with Stuart. Then I was left alone again to contemplate how a single unpremeditated act of generosity, and the taste of nourishing food, could so change a person's entire perspective, if only for a quarter of an hour, before returning, bored senseless, to my study of Italian's saltier expressions of endearment.

The following day, in the yard, Marco asked if I would be willing to take a letter out with me, assuming that I was soon to be granted my freedom. He was genial and persuasive, and I could see little harm in helping him. Moreover, I could see no good reason why I would be searched going *out* of the prison, so I accepted, and he surreptitiously slipped me a folded sheet of paper, telling me there was a phone number written on the blank side. I was to call this number and wait for a woman called Barbara to meet me in a bar, the address of which I memorized. As if providence had moved in accordance with Marco's prediction, in the early afternoon, Stuart and I were called out of our cells, and taken to an office on the ground floor of the building. An obese man with a pencil moustache, dressed in an expensive-looking silk suit, greeted us cordially and informed us, in the most civil terms, in American English, that we had committed no crime (as if a minor matter, the security of the civil population clearly being of greater concern than our personal liberty, a notion with which we were by now manifestly acquainted), but warned us that Sicily was perhaps not the ideal destination for us, and we should think about taking ourselves elsewhere, possibly somewhere on the Italian mainland, but not Sicily, and certainly not Messina. We all shook hands, and Stuart and I, unchastened but relieved, were escorted to collect our belongings. I carried the letter in my jeans pocket, having decided that the best policy, if searched, would be to feign total innocence of having transgressed any law. The worst that could happen was that they might confiscate the letter, but that was a risk of which Marco and I were aware. Hiding it, for example, in my anus, would have implied some kind of guilt. Besides, I had read the note, which was in Italian, and unless a secret code was embedded in the text, there was nothing that was incriminating; no names were mentioned other than the addressee's, and the function of the note was simply to inform Barbara of Marco's whereabouts, and to contact certain other people (she would, the note said, know who). For my part, I was more than a little intrigued to see what might happen when we met up with Barbara, whoever she was.

We found the bar without difficulty and had just enough change for a beer apiece. I made the call. We waited. Stuart made lewd and disrespectful conjecture about the possible outcome of our meeting with Barbara, whom he clearly imagined would fit some absurd stereotype of a gangster's moll, perhaps suggested to him by a week in which his only company and intellectual nourishment for twenty-three hours a day had been a collection of lurid pornography.

Barbara did not live up to Stuart's expectations. She was no gangster's moll, but a conservatively dressed and very serious young woman, who braced herself visibly before reading Marco's note and then sighed loudly, looking around the bar as though in an effort to will herself out of the company she had fallen into. It was a nondescript bar in a poor part of town. I could sense her anxiety, the shadow of a certain weariness about her eyes; she sighed again, asked a few questions in a reluctant monotone, and I was relieved when she turned to go, leaving her coffee half-finished on the counter.

Given that we had nowhere else to go, Stuart and I set out for the peace camp at Comiso, to do our bit against the Cold War.

Several months later, while staying at the Villa Ranchetti in Florence, I read an article in *La Repubblica* concerning the sentencing of Marco S, allegedly the key figure in a major international drugs ring. Without knowing it, I had acted as messenger for the Howard Marks of the Sicilian underworld.

18

I am reading Nabokov's *Speak, Memory*, the writer's account of his first forty years, and am struck by a passage in which he claims that one of his earliest recollections is of travelling on "the long-extinct Mediterranean Train de Luxe" and of "seeing with an inexplicable pang, a handful of fabulous lights that beckoned to me from a distant hillside, and then slipped into a pocket of black velvet: diamonds that I later gave away to my characters to alleviate the burden of my wealth." Despite the Nabokovian hyperbole, I fully recognise the memory as my own, while travelling as a child down the Italian *autostrada* in the family car; passing at speed below those hillside villages, and feeling the thrill of wonderment, the never-to-be-revealed mysteries of whoever lived in those illuminated dwellings, each pinprick of light indicating a living cell, each one a home filled with people whose lives were utterly hidden, yet visible to me through the metaphor of a shining electric bulb. The transience of the vision was made emphatic, more final, when another dark hill loomed, barring the distant cluster of lights from my line of vision.

Years later, travelling on a Greek ferry from Paros to Piraeus, we called in, at dusk, on the island of Naxos. Pulling into the harbour, the street lamps announcing the fall of night, I was stricken by a profound stillness, and a sadness that this moment would never be repeated – the same sadness that I recognise in the poetry of Cavafy – that never again would I sail into this harbour at dusk with the muted shouts of stevedores and the calling of gulls and the heaviness in the heart that only lost or ailing love can inflict, and the knowledge that, with time, all this marvellous fading luminosity, too, would be dimmed to nothing.

19

One sunny morning in July 1986 I was sitting on the terrace of a café in Alikes, on the island of Zakinthos. I had known the place before the tourist boom and had come back after meeting and selling melons with a young islander in Patras, who offered me work on his father's farm. When the melon harvest finished, I decided to stay for the rest of the summer. It was the closest I ever came to being an authentic beach bum. I found regular employment, first renting out lounger beds and pedalos to tourists, and then as a gardener – not that I had much experience, but I probably knew more than anyone else in the village, or at least could be bothered to muddy my knees and talk to the plants. There was a row of holiday homes fronting the beach, owned by islanders who had emigrated to Melbourne or Toronto and returned for a month over the summer. One person asked me to do some weeding, I suggested a couple of structural improvements to her garden, next thing the whole street wanted to employ me. So I did gardening in the mornings, and also had a cushy job with one of the tour operators in the afternoon a couple of times a week, furnishing holiday apartments with hospitality packs, a job that involved doing a circuit of the chalets with local delicacies (mineral water, a bottle of retsina, some vile Greek confectionery). The second job took me an hour, for which I was generously paid by Cathy, the tour company rep, who found in me someone to confide the dreadful secrets of her package tour charges and her own tragically predictable sexual exploits with the island studs, or *kamakia* (the singular form of the word, shamefully, means 'harpoon').

So I was getting up early and keeping busy. Thanks to regular swimming and walking I was reasonably fit. If I had been tempted, there was even the promise of a holiday romance with some sun-seeking tourist looking for a diversion from swarthy Greek harpoons. Coachloads of these holidaymakers turned up each week from the airport and I would listen in on their conversations as they drank themselves into oblivion in the beach bars; they would talk about the characters in television soaps and discuss English football. The teenagers listened to pop music on a thing called a Walkman. Hearing these people talk, watching them roast to a lobster pink before falling asleep in the sun and having to be hospitalised for heatstroke, I learned that the fashions, cultural trends and latest music from the UK were not only things unknown, but held no interest for me.

I had stayed in a neighbouring village the previous winter, and worked in the olive oil factory. The factory owner loaned me a room for the summer. I had a few books of poetry and history and an illustrated natural history of the plants and fauna of the Mediterranean. I liked sitting at the edge of the sea with my feet in water, looking over the calm bay. In the evening I played cards in the *kafeneion*. I was almost entirely lacking in ambition.

As I sat there finishing my omelette and fresh orange juice, and the waitress brought me a cappuccino, my friend Fadi ambled onto the terrace. Fadi had an interesting story. He had arrived in Marseilles on the Tunis ferry as a very young man some twelve years earlier, with little French and a lot of hashish. He was stopped by customs officers and spent the first two years of his European adventure in a French prison. Here he made good use of his time. He took advantage of prisoner training schemes to study language and literature, reading everything that he could find in the prison library. He read philosophy and history and fiction. On release from prison he settled in Paris and engaged in minor criminal activity for a number of years, but something bad happened which encouraged him to start travelling, and he had travelled ever since, not always passing frontiers in the conventional manner. Fadi drank, and could be a handful, but I had known him for four years and he remained one of my closest friends. He ordered Greek coffee and a brandy.

"Bonjour. What brings you to the seaside?" I asked. "Are you building sandcastles? Or are your intentions of a more sinister nature?"

"I have a job on a building site, a hotel. The guy said he'd meet me here at eight. That thing over there." He pointed at a square cement construct with iron rods poking from the roof.

"So right, sandcastles. Your man was playing cards till four this morning. He won't be here till ten."

Fadi looked at the remnants of my omelette with distaste, raised an eyebrow.

"What manner of breakfast is that?" he asked.

"Eggs. Orange juice. Coffee with milk. I lack only a croissant."

"Pah! That is not a vagabond's breakfast. That is the breakfast of a bourgeois. There is only one breakfast for the likes of you and me: garlic sausage, a litre of rouge and the open road."

We were talking in French. For the open road Fadi used the phrase *les grands chemins*, literally 'the big roads'.

I put down my fork and considered whether or not this was a coincidence. *Les Grands Chemins* was the title of a novel by Jean Giono that I had recently read about a gentle, hard-working, hard-drinking itinerant labourer who teams up with a trickster character, a man referred to as 'the artist', who performs astounding card tricks. The two of them wander around the villages and forests of what I imagined to be Provence. But the artist is a man who likes to play with fire, who will risk everything in the intensity of the moment and in the novel it is pretty much a certainty that he will come to a bad end, lending the story the characteristics of a Greek tragedy. It is a book infused with ironic good humour and delight in the simple pleasures of food and wine, and written entirely in the present tense. It had immediately been promoted to my list of favourite novels, but Fadi did not know this.

"You are trying to categorise me, my friend. There are many types of vagabond, and many kinds of breakfast. One hat does not fit every head."

"And you are eating an omelette and drinking orange juice. I am disappointed. You have become a *bourgeois*, with your little gardening trowel and your tourist rep girlfriend. I always considered you *plus Gainsbourg que Gainsbourg*."

"You flatter me."

"You are welcome. But you should maintain your standards. Currently you are exhibiting bad faith."

I looked at Fadi with a steady eye. I knew his game. Evidently it dismayed him to see me indulging in the sober comforts of a healthy breakfast. Addicts get upset if they suspect a fellow addict of letting the side down.

"Don't worry yourself, you miserable Arab felon," I said. "It won't last. We will soon both be skint and homeless once again."

I knew this to be the case, but I intended to enjoy my few days of sanity and peace. I became bored very easily. Boredom was compounded by a generic and unspecified anger. It was almost a point of honour for me to be recurrently enraged at the world. And if I hung around the same place for long, something would usually provoke it. I knew that however content I might appear today, working as a gardener and eating my eggs, sooner or later I would insult somebody or engineer some appalling row, about which I would likely remember nothing, and I would wake the next day or the one after that lying in a ditch and craving the vagabond's breakfast and the open road, and Fadi and I would set out with the sun on our faces and the wind at our backs. This constant churning dissatisfaction, this need to be always ready to move on, it was not a Romantic preoccupation, nor the idealisation of an ever-elusive elsewhere; it was simply a hazard of lifestyle – ultimately, it was a choice.

20

September 1986. I woke in the blackness beneath a swaying, star-filled sky. Someone was pulling my shoulder, gently at first, and then more roughly, as, with an effort, I struggled towards consciousness. I was cold, dressed only in a pair of shorts, lying on the bare wooden deck of what appeared to be a moving, sea-borne vessel. The men waking me were not wearing uniform. I was tucked into a concealed space beneath a lifeboat. I had no idea how I had got here; nor had I any idea what ship this was, nor what sea I was on, nor, for the first moments, in what language I should address the men.

I was escorted to the skipper's cabin and discovered that the ship was bound for Alexandria, but would make for port at Kastelli, in western Crete, where I would be put ashore. I was given a blue pullover and a pair of trainers. One of the sailors kindly brought me a coffee. I was worn out and half-drunk. My body felt like it had been run over by a truck, my flesh was covered in strange wounds and abrasions.

As soon as we touched land, I fell victim to an attack of persistent, restless gloom, as though I had relinquished all autonomy and events were overtaking me with some malicious intent. My arrival on the suspiciously hospitable ship, my being woken during a night crossing with no notion of my destination, these were very bad signs. I hitched a lift into Hania, borrowed some money from an Egyptian fishing friend, Karim, and spent the day moping about town, visiting old haunts, and sitting up on the Venetian battlements overlooking the harbour. I felt a weariness and nostalgia for the time I lived in the town under happier circumstances, sharing a house in the Splanzia quarter with an Argentinian fellow traveller, Cacho Fricker. We found the house through Peter Green (of whom more later) and after a month of bachelor debauch, we were joined by Loretta, a twenty-one year old British Somali girl, and her friend Lynne, who were backpacking around the islands and had made a fateful stop one evening at the restaurant where Cacho and I were eating. The four of us made up the perfect ingredients for a D.H. Lawrence novel, set by the Greek sea.

That summer was a time of rare discoveries, of strong friendships and intense pleasures. Still smarting from my break-up with Natasha, I saw my move to Hania as a new beginning. I had money in the bank, I was free from the snarling misery of London under the reign of the Iron Lady, and the sun shone brightly every day. I was, for a while, genuinely happy. I bought a seven-metre fishing boat, and made lazy excursions down the coast, dropping anchor in isolated bays, and attempting, with limited success at first, to catch fish. Loretta and I took long walks in the White Mountains where we would hike for days and sleep out under the stars. The nights were long and our hearts were full. Needless to say, it didn't last. While Cacho and Lynne stayed together and later had two sons, Loretta and I split up within a few months, after I made an urgent trip to London to help sort out a crisis with Natasha – not the wisest decision of my life.

Although my affair with Loretta ended in acrimony and accusation and she moved in with her new Greek boyfriend, she at least had the decency to bail me out of the local jail a few months later for the theft of a mule; a clear case of mistaken identity to everyone apart from the arresting officer. But our relationship set a template for the other women I tried to live with over the next decade (and not only in setting a precedent for a series of romantic liaisons with women of Caribbean or African descent). However promising, however passionate the outset of an affair, sooner or later the realisation would dawn on my partner that she had taken on my obsession with alcohol as part of the package. I became living evidence of the axiom that addicts don't have relationships – they take hostages. I spent the next nine years zigzagging from one doomed entanglement to the next, and appearing to care less and less as the years went by (indeed for periods of time, in France, the level of my social dereliction took me to zones where the few available women were either incontinent or permanently brain-damaged).

In matters of the heart the monomania and blindness of the addict know no bounds, even as his self-aggrandisement and sense of loss are convoluted and blown out of all proportion. As Marguerite Duras suggested, the heartbreak of the drunk – like all his emotions – demands to be godlike and excessive in its glory and its despair. In emotional terms, the addict crossed in love resembles the doormat at the centre of the universe.

I returned to the Splanzia that first night and stayed in a house rented by German travellers, one of whom, Jochen, I had known since that first full year in Hania, five years back in 1981. In the small hours, I was standing on the parapet that surrounded the flat roof of his house, overlooking a small, cobbled square three stories below. There was a pile of gravel to the side, and a cement mixer, loosely covered in tarpaulin. I had a clear notion that I was swaying. I must have climbed onto the parapet while still in blackout and, with a start, had awoken between swaying motions, feeling the lure of gravity and knowing that within a second or two I would be lying in a crumpled heap on the concrete below. Hands grabbed me firmly from behind, holding me around the chest, and lifted me back onto the terrace. Jochen, a bear-like pirate, inspected me briefly and said:

"You looking to take a dive?"

I nodded, confused. What had I been doing up there? What strange and perverse instinct led me to these actions, in which I was not capable of conscious speech or thought but seemed able to move around and put myself into suicidal situations? I resembled a zombie at such times, a man who has lost his soul, or at least relinquished all control over his faculties of reason. And yet, at certain moments, snatched at rare intervals, the alcoholic is subject to a sudden revelation of razor-sharp acuity – the famous moment of clarity – in which the order of things makes perfect sense, and I was granted one that night on Jochen's roof, contemplating my surroundings with a scintillating intelligence, even though I knew that a microsecond's delay would send me tumbling from the rooftop. For years I had suffered from recurring nightmares about falling from a great height: what clearer warning could I have received of my overreaching and grandiosity – and of the imminent danger of a fall? However, once that moment of clarity had passed – and with it the potential for making a life-altering decision – I was confronted by an ever-deepening chasm of twisted and disintegrating thoughts, and could hear only the echoing of footsteps on the cobbled street below. The incident served as a reminder of the seemingly obvious (but easily forgotten) notion that one might die at any given moment. It was merely an act of chance that Jochen had appeared behind me, and I had survived. I took this knowledge with me, although I was not sure quite what to do with it. In some strange way, it reassured me.

Two years later, I heard that Jochen himself had died of alcohol-related liver disease. He was barely thirty.

A week or so into my stay in Hania, I fell ill. I had no blanket or sleeping bag and the nights were becoming cold. I remember – or seem to remember – being picked up from the street and taken into a yard behind some buildings near the harbour, being told to lie down on an old mattress. Someone was speaking English with an impossible, strangulated accent, half-reprimanding, half-concerned. Whoever it was, they threw a blanket over me. I fell into a feverish sleep, a nightmarish zone of terrible images and sublime fear. I don't know how long I stayed there, in the yard. There was a flimsy wooden construct behind me and partly above me, rather like a fruit stall, so that at least my head and upper body were in the shade when daylight arrived. But I was unable to move; I attempted to get up but fell over, and I lay there sweating and mumbling and falling into a half-dream state which lasted throughout the day and the following night. I have vague memories of someone checking on me from time to time, and hearing two people talking quietly and insistently; one of them seemed to be a child or adolescent. To add to my confusion, they were speaking in French.

"*Ne t'inquiète pas, mon brave; c'est un vagabond.*"

"*Un vagabond? C'est quoi ça?*"

"*C'est quelqu'un sans domicile.*"

I turned over to try and catch a glimpse of the intruders, to see who had taken it upon himself to explain the basics of homelessness, but they had vanished into the night. *Vagabond.* So that's what I am, I thought, savouring the taste of this identity, which has a vaguely Romantic affiliation, more so in a French enunciation. On another occasion I heard voices discussing whether or not to try and get me to the hospital. I heard the word pneumonia. However, in spite of the state I was in, I had no intention of allowing anybody to take me to a hospital.

Three or four days after first collapsing, emaciated and drenched in sweat, I dragged myself from the sodden mattress and managed to step out of the yard, blinking in the sunlight. I stumbled into Michalis' taverna, where I had once been employed as waiter, and headed for the toilets. The mirror reflected back a face that was haggard and wild, with one cheek horribly engorged. I was going to have to do something about the toothache.

I managed to blag some medication off a pharmacist, which helped a bit, and cut down on drinking for a couple of days. Michalis gave me free meals. I remember hanging out with a bunch of real lowlife at this time. They all depressed me, including those who, I assumed, had helped me by providing the filthy mattress under the broken wooden shelter. In his book *Montano*, Enrique Vila-Matas writes: "Deep down I am horrified by stupid, drunken arguments between tramps, and even more by the places where they live." How true this was of my own miserable plight. What depths of self-loathing were plumbed during those times of penury and hand-to-mouth survival. My associates got drunk every day, beginning early, and by evening were raucous and vile; they horrified me, with their absurd, drunken arguments, their lives of useless conjecture, and my disgust was heightened by the realisation that I was no different from them.

Michalis' taverna was actually called *To Diporto*, meaning The Two Doors. The restaurant no longer exists, though whether it was closed for reasons of health and safety I do not know: it certainly should have been. It is now a gift shop, run by Michalis' son. But the place acquired a status in my unconscious as a zone of eternal return, and for many years afterwards I would dream about *To Diporto*, finding myself in an oneiric Hania and having to seek it out, vainly scouring the streets and alleys of the town, only to find that it was no longer there, or that it was but had shifted location, changing its shape and its décor, constantly evading me.

This taverna could be found half way down Skridlov Street, the narrow thoroughfare that is lined by shops selling leather goods, for which reason it is known to locals and foreigners alike as Leather Street. I had wandered into the place on my first night in Hania, back in 1981, and as soon as I set foot inside, I knew that this dingy, badly-lit, anarchic, cramped and disreputable little taverna lived up to my notions of the ideal drinking-den. The food was basic: a predictable range of fish and seafood, liver, pig gonads and chops. There was no moussaka and there were no desserts. The wine was strong and rough. The owner, Michalis Kostakis, was sly and endearing. At night, several tables lined the narrow pavement outside the front: these were usually taken by carousing travellers, the post-punk detritus of northern Europe and stoned hippies who had got lost on their way back from India. The narrow front room held six or seven tables, a large display fridge, and boasted a single piece of artwork: a print of the parachute landings during the battle of Crete, in which a swarthy old Cretan was taking a swipe at a descending German paratrooper with an outsized shepherd's crook. Michalis worked behind the stove in a little kitchen recess which overlooked both the front room and a section of the restaurant that lay at a slightly lower level and boasted an antique jukebox. The remainder of the clientele consisted of Greek naval conscripts carrying out their obligatory thirty-month military service, American naval personnel from the base at Souda Bay, assorted maniacs and oddballs, and local scrapings of the underworld, notably prostitutes from the Splanzia district and their pimps. One regular was a sixty-year-old German survivor of the parachute drop of 1941 with a weakness for pigs' balls, who had returned to buy a holiday home in the land he had invaded as a young man. *I was loving Creta from the first time I have come,* he told me, unabashed.

It was a cosmopolitan brew of customers, and I got to know most of them over the couple of years I lived in Hania. When busy, it was a festive, bustling place, but that first night – my first in Hania – *To Diporto* was quiet. It was past midnight and unless a group of free-spending sailors turned up, Michalis would be closing up before long. I chose a table in the almost deserted front room, and sat staring at the walls and ceiling, which were of an indistinguishable colour, their original tone obscured over the years by a dirty ochre overlay of cigarette smoke.

A waiter approached my table. He was a small man with a drooping blonde-grey moustache, clear blue eyes, and a peculiar, shuffling gait in which the feet were not permitted to leave the floor. I guessed he was in his thirties. He was certainly not a Greek. I ordered ouzo and a *meze*, having to repeat my order, since the waiter appeared to be deaf in one ear. This man was Peter Green, an English drop-out and professional drunk, who would shortly become my neighbour. He reminded me of the English junkie played by John Hurt in *Midnight Express*. Peter spoke English with the inflections of a smart education and was the scruffiest human being imaginable, but these were no deterrent to his holding the position of waiter in an establishment as downbeat as *To Diporto*. He was an inspired and inventive source of information about all things Cretan, as well as classical mythology, the history of the Balkans, twentieth-century Turkish poetry and Tottenham Hotspur football club; and because of his privileged position as waiter in Michalis' dive, one of the first people to get hold of local gossip, to hear of comings and goings, and to learn of police activity in the town. He was a fabulous raconteur, and entirely unreliable. We spent a lot of time together, both in Crete and France.

But on this later occasion, in the autumn of 1986, Peter was no longer the waiter at *To Diporto*. He had been, around this time, as I discovered later, locked up in a psychiatric hospital in Seville, from which he escaped, clad only in pyjamas, no doubt in search of a quiet drink, before being hunted down by a posse of nurses and returned, strait-jacketed, to his ward.

Peter was an impossible alcoholic but also a gentle soul, one of nature's gentlemen, who would never consciously have caused harm to another living being. His death in Athens in 1988 caused me great sadness, but came as no surprise. His grasp on life had always seemed tenuous.

After one of my nocturnal adventures on this return trip I too ended up in hospital. I had, during the past four years of aimless travel, visited many accident and emergency units on several occasions, in different countries, but I usually had an inkling as to what had brought me there. On this occasion I had none. I retained a vague memory of walking past one of the night clubs in a side street off the harbour front, and the next thing I knew I was lying in a hospital bed, my head swathed in bandages from a nasty wound to the crown. I was able to piece together the latter part of my escapade with the help of one of the nurses. She explained to me that I had been brought in by a young

Cretan who said he was a friend of mine. The duty registrar (or rather, the nurse informed me, his assistant, a medical student) attempted to stitch up my head-wound. Unfortunately, he had accidentally nicked the main vessel traversing the skull, causing a fountain of blood to burst from my head and cascade down onto both of us. I had no idea who my mystery escort was, but guessed it might have been Nikos Makrinakis, a friend from the old days, since the nurse had said he was tall and handsome.

When I got dressed, preparing to leave the hospital the next day, I discovered, to my surprise, that I had enough money to eat and drink, so set off, head extravagantly bandaged, for Mama's restaurant, a dive as downmarket as *To Diporto*, set back in the street of knife grinders behind the harbour. Mama's was very cheap, and the eponymous owner gave no credit. She ran the place on her own, specialising in bean soup and *keftedes* (a variety of flattened meatball) which tasted of sawdust and gristle. Despite the fact that we were paying customers, Mama's place had the feel of a charity soup kitchen, and attracted an appropriate clientele. It was never exactly cosy, but there was a cave-like sense of having arrived somewhere *essential* about its dark, bare interior. Outside, and up crumbling whitewashed steps, could be found the most terrifying of Greek toilets in a country which boasted serious competition. Considering the impact that Greek lavatorial facilities tend to have on even the most robust of constitutions, remarkably little has been written about them. Don DeLillo, in his novel *The Names*, is an exception: "It was the terminal shithouse of the Peloponnese. The walls were splattered with shit, the bowl was clogged, there was shit on the floor, on the toilet seat, on the fixtures and pipes. An inch of exhausted piss lay collected around the base of the toilet, a minor swamp in the general wreckage and mess... [T]his doleful shed was another plane of experience. It had a history, a reek of squatting armies, centuries of war, plunder, siege, blood feuds."

I struggled to keep down my host's meatballs, had her fill a large plastic bottle with fierce tawny wine, and escaped to my spot on the Venetian battlements overlooking the harbour.

That evening, dishevelled and argumentative, I wound up on the outskirts of town, and managed to get involved in a bar brawl. My assailant was a Belgian whom I knew vaguely, and had never liked; nor, as I soon discovered, did he much care for me. I forget the precise nature of our altercation, but I do remember that he called me a parasite, which stung, and I retaliated by saying something quite rude to him in French, to which he took particular offence. Admittedly, I had already regurgitated the remains of Mama's meatballs into his lap, but in spite of my clearly handicapped status as walking wounded, I was cast ignominiously out of the bar by the Belgian and one of his cronies, and lay on the roadside covered in bruises and vomit and blood, like the character in the Johnny Cash song, before crawling into a field of bamboo and passing out.

In the morning I wandered a couple of miles back towards Hania and found a quiet beach. I needed a drink but had spent the last of my money the night before. I lay on the sand and stared at the sea. Off to my left, a young couple were enjoying the autumn sun. As I absentmindedly stared at them, the girl wriggled out of her jeans and, raising her hips, reached down to pull on bikini pants. That brief moment, in which she lay back, naked from the waist down, hoisting her buttocks like a gymnast, instilled in me an awful, hopeless, surge of erotic longing, compounded by the cascade of hormonal activity that always seemed to accompany a comedown from alcohol; the ease of her movement, the wanton look she cast at her boyfriend, the uncomplicated pleasure they sought in each other's company, so life-affirming, so gracious: it made me shudder.

I found a bar and had a wash in the bathroom. I had managed to exchange my shorts for tattered and greasy army pants. My blue jersey, a gift from the ship's skipper, was torn at the neck and splattered with colourful stains. My sneakers had disappeared somewhere and been replaced by plastic fisherman's sandals. I was very tanned, but my face was blotchy and swollen, and there were patches of dried skin on my cheeks and between my horribly bloodshot eyes, one of which was also blackened, or rather ripening into a state of purple splendour, and the bandage around my head bore the muddy marks of a night spent in a field. Leaving the bathroom, I discarded this last article in a garbage bin, removed the filthy gauze dressing, and set off down the road back towards Hania.

I had not gone far when a pick-up truck pulled in alongside me. A squat, muscular man with the face of a pugilist leaned over to address me. He spoke, alarmingly, in Midwestern American, augmented by Greek inflections. You want work? he enquired. I mumbled in noncommittal fashion and settled into the passenger seat, relieved for the ride, but with no intention of taking up his offer. He looked me over as he drove. You're all fucked up, he observed, astutely. You been in a fight? I did not wish to recount the various acts of violence that my body had endured over the past few days. Shortly before entering Hania he turned off towards the beach, and parked outside an ugly concrete edifice, which, he informed me, was his hotel. Apart from the ground floor, it had a long way to go before becoming habitable, but, to my amazement, he offered me work as a building labourer. It occurred to me that the man was out of his mind: at that moment I must have been the least employable person on the island under the age of ninety. Every morning there were hordes of able-bodied young men queuing up for jobs outside Café Costas in the harbour square: why pick on me? I became suspicious. He showed me around. I remained unimpressed. It was the usual botch-job; pile on the cement and hope for the best. I had worked on half a dozen of these sites in Greece; but I was fitter then, and the last couple of years had done nothing for my stamina. I was about to walk away when he showed me a clean, bare room on the ground floor, complete with a soft bed and ensuite bathroom, and told me I would be staying here while working for him. I took the job.

The first day's work nearly finished me off. My new employer had me heaving sacks of cement up staircases, while he yelled vulgar, macho abuse at me on account of my poor physique. He had spent fifteen years in Chicago and had returned home in order to take advantage of the booming tourist industry. His half-built hotel was a disgrace, even by the standards of the Greek construction industry. I imagined he had run out of cash, otherwise he would have employed proper builders rather than derelicts from the roadside; he clearly didn't have a clue what he was doing. I had never worked for such an inept boss. He attempted to set up a small pulley device to lift a wheelbarrow from one floor to the next, but the thing collapsed almost immediately. His cement mixer kept breaking down because the leads to his makeshift generator were faulty. He showed me how strong he was by lifting two fifty kilogram sacks of cement up several flights of stairs, then rolled his tee shirt sleeve up to the armpit to pose for me, flexing his muscles like some idiot body-builder. I wondered if he might be gay. Much of the time he kept up a stream of scatological observations on life, politics, and my physical shortcomings – *look at ya man, yer arms are like marshmalla.* The ceaseless flow of obscene expletives was nothing new – this was, after all, a building site – but they always sound strange when uttered in a foreign accent. Moreover, for such a he-man, he had a rather squeaky, girlish voice, so all his fucks and assholes and motherfuckas ended up sounding vaguely comic. At one point I could restrain myself no more, and burst into hysterical laughter, doubled up under my sack of cement, which slid off my shoulder to the ground. He picked up the sack, glanced at me and said, "You're fuckin nuts, man." When work finally ended for the day I went straight to my room, collapsed on the bed in a heap, and fell asleep. I woke at ten in the evening and went out in search of food. The gangster had grudgingly given me a sub. A small taverna provided me with bean soup and a litre of red wine. I went back to my room and slept again, through till seven the next morning.

I stayed in the half-built hotel for nearly a week. The gangster was offering me a pittance, but I was staying out of trouble, eating two square meals a day, and was so exhausted at the end of each day's work that I lacked the energy to go adventuring in Hania in the evening. Besides, I had plenty of creditors there, and was not in a position to pay them back. However, on the Saturday, Chicago told me that we would not be working the next day, that I was to take the Sunday off. He gave me a thin wad of notes, deducting two thousand drachmae for a pair of trousers he had given me earlier in the week. In total, the wages came to less than a half of what I had been earning as a tomato-picker in the Pelopponese, but he was not the kind of employer you wrangle with. I had no possessions other than the clothes I was standing in, so, after a shower, I got on the bus into Hania, certain, despite the modest comforts of my room, that I would not be returning. That same night I jumped on the night ferry to Piraeus.

I spent the next three months homeless in Athens. It was the coldest winter for forty years and I remember waking one morning in a ruined building in the Plaka (the same roofless dwelling that would act as home to Peter, before his death) to see the Acropolis dusted with snow. The temperature stayed around zero for weeks on end, and I survived on a diet of cheap brandy, *Ethnos* cigarettes, and by cadging food vouchers off the students at the *Polyteknika*, who were, by and large, remarkably sympathetic. The days passed in a kind of slow delirium, trying to sleep at night in the waiting room of the train station, where at least there were radiators. Unfortunately the station was raided regularly by the police, so nights were often interrupted by a spell in the local slammer. There followed a much better month in Thessalonika and eventually I straightened myself out enough to find a couple of nights' work unloading trucks at the city market. With the money, I caught a bus through Yugoslavia to Milan, and hitched into France.

In my diary for 2004, when I had returned to Hania to do some research for the novel I was writing, I find these words: "I am revisiting a place in which all the leading characters are either lost or gone for ever, and I am like a ghost tracing the disappearance of their tracks."

Not only had I completely forgotten how to speak Greek, as though my capacity for the language had sloughed from me like an old skin, rendering me inarticulate for all but the most basic transactions, but eighteen years on Hania had evolved into the kind of place it had previously resisted becoming: a tacky, mass-market resort. I had made the mistake in my visits to the island, after 1982, of trying to re-invent the past, of attempting to recapture the paradisiacal narrative of my earlier sojourns there, when I lived in the shepherd's hut at Keratokambos, or my shared Splanzia house in 1981; but the truth was that nothing can be recaptured, nothing can be retained. I had failed to absorb one of the most basic lessons to be learned by the vagabond: *never go back*. Only an idiot could begin to imagine that the past can be trapped and reiterated; only a person wholly deceived by the lure of nostalgia, which Lawrence Durrell called the loveliest of Greek words, could so delude himself.

21

A human flotsam, a flow of itinerant labour followed familiar routes around the orchards and vineyards of southern Europe, its members occasionally finding odd jobs on campsites, on construction sites or in dingy bars and restaurants, or selling drinks and ice creams on the summer beaches.

Among the group of vagabonds with whom I consorted during the 1980s there would be a general migration to France in the summer and autumn, in order to work on the cherries, the peaches and the maize in Languedoc and Gascony, followed by the grape harvest, the *vendange* (I favoured Corbières, but also spent one season in the Cognac region). After the *vendange*, many of us would venture down to Spain for a while, where the exchange rate meant that French francs went a long way, and in December there would be a migration back to Greece (in my case Crete, or the Pelopponese) for the olives and the oranges. I also worked in several restaurants in Greece, as a waiter, where my languages came in handy – I had a facility for learning a new language *in situ*, a talent I have never displayed in the classroom – but never for very long, as I had a habit of upsetting the customers. There were variations on this pattern, of course, and as the decade progressed my migrations became more and more erratic, and I spent more time in Spain. I picked up Spanish the same way I learned other languages – the street, newspapers and television – but supplemented my vocabulary at first by reading Bukowski in translation.

Sifting this afternoon through the few notebooks that remain from the 1980s, all of them horribly stained and tattered, it is extraordinary how much time I wasted sitting around, waiting for something to happen, living in abandoned buildings in Greece and Italy, staying in flophouses for the homeless in France and Spain, or, more usually, sleeping rough. I endured long periods with no money and little food, working a few days here or there, getting drunk for days or weeks at a time; was hospitalised in four countries for detox, as well as for a staggering assortment of injuries, including an impressive number of head-wounds following incidents in which I was hit by people or moving vehicles. Once, in a pub called Flanagan's Tower, in Walthamstow, which for all I know still stands, I was dragged outside by the landlord, a burly, homicidal fellow – no doubt I had offended him with some item of sarcasm or personal derogation, behaviours I have sought to contain over the years – who grasped my head and battered it repeatedly against the outer wall of the hostelry, putting me at risk of all manner of cerebral injuries. But this was only one in a series of such assaults.

Despite my early close encounter with drowning, I developed a strong predilection for immersing myself in water: among the rivers of France, I have swum in the Aveyron, Charente, Dordogne, Gers, Tarn, Léez, Arros and Bidasoa rivers, and have jumped or fallen inebriated into the Adour and the Garonne, and once I dived spectacularly and from a great height into the Lot, another of the great rivers of France. On a rare visit to England I fell, or rather rolled into the River Severn at Shrewsbury, whereupon I was taken to the psychiatric hospital and shut up in a locked ward on suspicion of being an attempted suicide, in spite of my protestations that suicide was not an option since, like Prometheus, I could not die – an argument which failed to convince the duty psychiatrist (glancing over at this doctor's notes while he answered a telephone call, I made out the dire terms – "delusional… drug addiction… chronic alcoholism… vagrancy" – that defined my status). Once I swam across a river whose name I forget, in order to avoid passing through customs between Yugoslavia and Greece because my travelling companion had no passport and was wanted by the Greek police, and on another occasion I carried a Cretan mountain dog called Tango across the roaring torrent that courses the depths of the Samaria Gorge in winter (I slipped – it was a case of dropping either the large bottle of ouzo I was carrying or the dog; the ouzo won – and the dog fell into the water, but I managed to catch hold of his tail before he was swept away: he glowered at me in sullen indignation after I had dragged him by this appendage to the bank). I was given to spontaneous late-night swimming on several occasions, especially if there was a small off-shore island within what appeared to be a manageable distance, though such excursions were always ill-advised.

Extreme behaviour wears a person out; all the biographical baggage that full-time drunks acquire, it seems so excessive and pointless to me now. There was nothing remotely heroic about this lifestyle. Many of my close friends died in their twenties or thirties: drink, drugs, suicide, AIDS; the usual litany. Not even these deaths were enough to stop me on my own chosen path.

But the single most resounding memory of the years spent as a vagabond are of immense tedium, waiting around for something to happen; the hours spent outside cafés nursing a single drink, of rendezvous with potential employers who never turned up, of having to listen to the interminably tedious advice of a certain breed of seasoned world-traveller, of the inane chatter of junkies and petty criminals, devising some crackpot scheme or other to get money, none of these plans ever materialising, or if they did, spending days in fear of an encounter with the police, or worse, some criminal element seeking them out to secure retribution for a wrong, real or imagined, committed by one of their number: one of *our* number, since, although not necessarily setting out to acquire companions on the road, one inevitably finds oneself with fellow-vagrants and outcasts, from all manner of backgrounds, and from many countries – in those days usually Spanish, Portuguese and North African, since the influx from eastern Europe had not yet begun – all out to get something for nothing, or for very little, along with the more earnest job-seekers. It is true to say that there was a certain camaraderie amongst the younger down-and-outs and we would often bump into each other in different municipal food kitchens across northern Spain or in Andalucia, where most of these dropouts would end up during the colder months. I spent only one winter there, in Granada, Almeria, and on the Cabo de Gato coast. I travelled with all kinds of people, of all ages: French, Italian, Spanish, German, Palestinian, Tunisian, Algerian, even a Russian asylum-seeker, Arkady, a classically-trained pianist, who worked the nightclubs in the ski resorts of Savoie, where I had gone to look for work.

Things would sometimes get nasty in France: among the more hardened *clochards*, the criminal element would occasionally surface, many of them carried knives, and these would be whipped out on the slightest pretext, but only once did I see a proper knife-fight, outside the dosshouse in Avignon, with two figures writhing on the ground, knives slashing, and a lot of blood. The Romani travellers had a bad reputation for violence, and I witnessed this for myself more than once, the most spectacular occasion being at Villeneuve-sur-Lot, when I had been picked up, along with two Irish travellers, Pearse and Colm, with an offer of work, picking plums. The entire morning had been spent in the back of a large white van, travelling from farm to farm, occasionally picking up or dropping off other Romani. I couldn't make out what kind of employment we were being offered, if any; the whole set-up was a shambles, and the leader of the clan, the driver, kept arguing with a woman in the front seat alongside him. Eventually we screeched to a halt on some street on the outskirts of town and the woman grabbed a hammer from the glove compartment and leaped out onto the pavement and began raining blows on the head of a passing woman, whom she had identified from her window seat as we drove along, the swings of the hammer accompanied with a flurry of abusive adjectives in a mix of Spanish and Romani. God knows what the poor woman was being accused of (other than being a slut and the daughter of a whore) but the hammer attack was sudden and vicious; she hit her on the head twice, three times, a sickening sound, and the woman slumped to the ground, by which time two of the men had jumped from the van also, including the driver, and were attempting to restrain the madwoman from doing any further damage, but she was completely out of control, shrieking and wailing, and trying to batter the other woman to death with her hammer. The men overpowered her, and the other woman was still struggling, her legs kicking, but I didn't see any more. Pearse, Colm and I escaped from the back of the van and legged it. It was clearly a bad direction, the idea of working with the gypsies, and although I was often asked to join a Romani team, on the plums or the peaches, or even the *vendange*, I was never tempted again. These people lived by another code entirely.

So much time spent hanging around, waiting either for work (which few of us actually wanted) or for the energy to move somewhere else, the eternal dilemma of the penniless vagrant: am I better off here, where I have nothing, but can secure two meals a day at the soup kitchen and a place to sleep for free in the local flophouse, or should I move on?

In places where there was not a municipal free restaurant or soup kitchen, I had a basic diet: bread (which could usually be acquired for nothing from a sympathetic bakery), garlic (which I had been told helped cleanse the blood) and tins of sardines (which could be easily slipped inside a pocket when the shopkeeper's back was turned) or some kind of dried sausage or cheese. Wine, obviously, was a priority, and since it was so cheap, one rarely had to go without. Cigarettes were another matter: they were cheap too, but you had to balance their purchase against the quantity of wine needed to get you through the day without going into withdrawal, and whether that left any change for tobacco. It seems I lived for several years on bread, garlic, sardines, red wine and black tobacco. Books, when I wanted to read, could always be stolen, or else perused in the warmth of a public library, a haven for tramps. Occasionally I would be overcome by some historical or literary obsession: Joan of Arc, the Crusades, the Cathars, Provençal poetry, the architecture of the early Romanic, García Lorca, the Spanish Civil War etc., and I would spend a few days reading things up in these hospitable places until my curiosity was sated, or I ran out of books on my pet obsession.

But the unending tedium of a hand-to-mouth existence gets to you in the end. You move on and end up doing the same thing in another place, another town, but at least the scenery is different for a while, and you get to meet a new bunch of vagabonds – who I would define as, generally speaking, younger dropouts, many of whom are perfectly intelligent and capable of finding a living for themselves in the real world, but choose not to, and some of whom (a small minority, thankfully) are psychopaths – and *clochards*, or local tramps, who often don't venture far beyond a defined neighbourhood, and tend to be older. Most of us were male, but among the vagabonds, as the decade passed, were a growing number of wild-eyed, dreadlocked girls, smelling, like their hippy precursors, of patchouli and marijuana.

22

San Sebastian. A grey Sunday afternoon in November. I was wandering unconcerned through the old town when I got caught up in a riot, one of the spontaneous outbreaks of violent protest that in those days were likely to erupt following a rally of Herri Batasuna, the radical Basque separatist party, which many Spanish politicians wished to ban, and later did. I heard a distant chanting, a crescendo of yells, and the ground started shaking. I turned a blind corner and a phalanx of police came tearing down the narrow cobbled street ahead of me with shields raised and truncheons swinging. Just ahead, a young woman in red was swaying towards the middle of the street, either challenging the oncoming stream of cops with ludicrous defiance, or else, I suspected, off her head on something. In a few seconds she would be beaten, crushed, trampled underfoot. I grabbed her, pulling her out of the path of the oncoming tide of blue, pressed her into a doorway. When the police had passed she turned and I recognised her as one of the girls from Plaza de la Trinidad – a favourite haunt of junkies and beggars – one of that tribe which in Spain I think of as the holy street urchins, the little acolytes of Saint Teresa. She had dirty blond hair, anthracite eyes; there were multi-coloured beads around her neck, silver bangles on her wrists and ankles, and she wore face paint, three horizontal crimson stripes on each cheek. She seemed to recognise me: after all, we frequented the same restaurant, or municipal soup kitchen. She breathed alcohol fumes in my face and smiled, but did not thank me for saving her from, at the very least, a severe battering.

We walked down to La Concha together, away from the demonstration, and along the seafront, which was buffeted by big waves that swept up against the prom, lashing the stonework and cascading over the paving stones. Charo turned out to be quite talkative, or at least she delivered an uninterrupted stream of consciousness monologue that seemed, at certain points, to be aimed at me. She had sobered up with the walk, or else had not been as out of it as I had thought. The weather was getting rough and I was planning to head up to the *Hogar de Transeúntes*, the flophouse, which is situated in a convent on the hill behind the exclusive Hotel Londres and where I would be able to get a hot meal and a bed. But Charo did not want to go there; she said she wanted to stay with me, and that in any case we could not take alcohol into the municipal hostel and she wanted to drink. She had some money, she told me. Let's stay out, *para emborracharnos y drogarnos* – in order to become drunk and to drug ourselves – she said, with an admirable clarity of intent. We slipped into a bar and watched the TV news reports on the afternoon's rally and police overreaction: it seemed a number of people had been badly injured and several vehicles burnt in the riot that followed the rally. The atmosphere in the old quarter was tense and expectant. A van filled with *Guardia Civil* made a circuit of Plaza de la Constitución. A few young men ran out of the bar to whistle and jeer at it. Later, the sense of anger and outrage, almost tangible when the van first hove into view, simmered down and was replaced by mutterings and exhortations of bravado. As night approached, the town was quiet and the streets almost empty.

We bought a big bottle of cheap muscatel and found a place to sit under the arches in the square. Paco, one of the kids from Plaza de la Trinidad, stopped by and gifted us a lump of hash, so we smoked a spliff and huddled close to keep warm. The rain was in abeyance but you could hear the wind howling through the narrow streets of the old town, names in Basque script on swaying signs, the indignant symbols of resistance. It is extraordinary how, during periods of civil unrest, the street people, the *clochards* and freaks and vagabonds and tramps and urban homeless all carry on as normal, as if all this political upheaval really had nothing to do with them.

Charo offered me pills. What are they, I asked, pills to make you weep? No, she said, laughing, pills to make you brave, pills that go with muscatel. I don't believe it, I said. They are pills to make your hair fall out, pills to make you grind your teeth. No, dickhead, said Charo, they are pills to make your balls drop off, and she laughed, delightfully.

We stayed out for a while longer then it got too cold so we found another bar where they knew Charo and we stayed there in the warm till closing time, and the pills began to take effect; I was feeling high and extremely brave, though I suspected in the morning my teeth would fall out after all; Charo was smiling in a way that suggested she was in possession of some wonderful secret which she was in no hurry to reveal. We picked up the *caritas* blankets she had stashed behind the bar, went out onto the square, grabbed an armload of cardboard from a skip, walked down a few streets and climbed a crumbling wall and through an archway without a streetlight nearby; this place is good, said Charo, this place is safe. We wrapped ourselves under the blankets and onto the card, she smelled like a warm animal, we burrowed deep into each other's warmth, deep into the soft haven of each other's sorrow, we lay under the canopy of night and listened to the wind tearing down the narrow streets of the city, listened to the howling of the wind in our warm and destitute embrace, until the drugs and sleep took us hostage, until sleep weighed down on us like mercury.

23

Edgar was an aspiring *clochard* in his late thirties, simple minded, a holy innocent, with the mournful face of a clown. He wandered the Charentes region doing agricultural work. But these young pickers, down at Cognac for the grapes, running out of things to do, had picked on him and shaved his head. They held him down while he was drunk, and gave him a Mohican haircut. And so he wore a black woolly hat, which made his clown's face all the sadder. Edgar joined us at the farm where we were picking grapes, and shared the outhouse where we cooked, ate and slept.

Edgar told us of his days doing military service. How he had to make a parachute jump, and looked out of the aeroplane in terror at the ground below. He saw, he said *les petits bonhommes* down below. He refused to jump. The sergeant pushed him anyway. It seemed to be what people did to Edgar, always.

That Sunday I went mushrooming with Edgar, who told me that he knew a thing or two concerning fungi. He knew nothing, and we returned with a sackful of inedibles. The farmer's wife picked through our findings with nimble fingers and one after another tossed all varieties aside, as Edgar's face drooped further still in disappointment. He later confided to me that what he *really* knew about was fishing. His father had taught him when he was a boy. Autumn in his village, people had gone hunting rabbits Sundays, or else mushrooming. But he and his father were exceptions: they were fishermen. Next Sunday, if we could only find some tackle, we would go fishing.

Edgar had very bad breath and evidently no notion of dental care. When one of the women told him he needed to do something about his oral hygiene he looked forlorn. The next morning I woke at half past six to see Edgar leaning over my bed, brushing vigorously, dribbling white foam. He gestured proudly with his free hand to show me that he had heeded the advice. He was cleaning his teeth with my toothbrush.

24

In the market square of Villeneuve-sur-Lot, now empty of vendors' stalls, sat a handsome young Arab, propped against a pillar, and shouting, or even singing, at whoever might be passing. He waved a bottle of red wine. People who passed that side of the square took a wide berth in order to avoid him; his drunkenness seemed quite volatile, as if about to explode into a violent display and no one wished to be in the immediate vicinity. I stayed in the shadows, on the other side of the square, under the cloisterish pillars, watching. I recognised him, and did not want him to see me, in case he engaged me in conversation.

I had not been listening to the young man's loud and garbled French. I assumed that it was not worth listening to. I heard it only as an unintelligible outpouring of sound: guttural, crude, with the impoverished grasp of grammar and limited vowel range common to many immigrant speakers of French from the Maghreb. But as time passed I realised that he was repeating the same utterance again and again. Gradually the words, slurred and broken by loud sobs of a psychotic intensity, took shape. He was proclaiming, to all who passed, his own immortality, laying claim to his place among the undying gods. *Je suis immortal!* He repeated the phrase again and again, louder and louder in the failing light of this sleepy, smug and rather uptight *municipalité*, reassuring the considerable population of *Front National* racists of the utterly despicable and richly deserved plight of The Arab. His words took on, to my ears at least, an intense spiritual beauty. I listened as his shouting, by turns wavering and croaky, powerful and raucous, attracted a police van, and I felt a sudden shared identity with this exotic young man, whose claims were undisputed, and whose single line would echo around the square long after the police had moved him on, like the canticle of a medieval sinner who spends all night in the stocks, humiliated, beaten, pelted with rotten food and human excrement, who rants his single loud ejaculation into the wilderness of dusk.

25

What becomes of those people we glance, in passing, and with whom we make some fleeting, momentary contact, perhaps never articulated in speech, or, if so, only a few words, a request, a direction given, or some face glimpsed in a crowd, or on a train, a sudden apprehension of some kind of empathy, a recognition of sorts? These people, and the courses that their lives take after they have disappeared from sight, fill me with a distressing yet beguiling sense of the transience of things, of the shades of possibility that undermine any belief in a solid and reliable constancy to our existence. Any one of them might become lifelong friends, or lovers, if only that silent glance were adumbrated with words, an invitation to share a coffee, to walk awhile along the strand. Or not. It all relates to what Kundera has famously called the unbearable lightness of being. These encounters usually, though not always, involve an erotic component, opening the gateway to an array of unfulfilled fantasies. But under most circumstances, social norms prohibit us from broaching the silence that separates us.

Before my illness took this turn for the worse, while staying at the house in Spain, I drove with friends across the border to Céret, three-quarters of an hour away, where there was an exhibition of paintings and ceramics by Chagall in the new museum, and a very fine gallery it is too, though when I say new, it has probably been there ten years or more. Anyway, I was standing outside the *Musée d'art moderne de Céret*, finishing a cigarette, when a blonde woman approached me, smartly-dressed, quite chic, in her mid-thirties, I would say, but looking sad and worn, as though something terrible had happened to her, or, more precisely, as though she carried with her the memory of some injury that she would not relinquish, and from which she would never recover. She had a face that would once have been pretty, and yet something had happened, and whatever it was had brutalised her, not to the extent, or in quite the same way, that a prostitute has been brutalised, dehumanized, not the extinguished eyes of the streetwalker, but her gaze exuded something approaching that degree of weary hurt. She asked me for a cigarette, she spoke softly, she addressed me as *monsieur*, in fact I almost didn't catch what she had said because her voice was so quiet, she must have thought I was alone, as my friends had gone in, and I, as I say, was finishing my cigarette outside, on my own. So I offered her a Camel and she took it, and there was a pause, in which I was expected to offer her a light, but for some reason I didn't, I turned and went inside the museum, leaving her outside with the unlit cigarette in her hand. It was only when I got inside, rejoined my friends, paid for my ticket, and began strolling past the exhibited works that I began to think about the little encounter outside. It was something about the way the woman had looked at me, a vulnerability and loneliness about her that was not solely to do with the submissive act of requesting a cigarette from a stranger, but the request had, it seemed to me, ulterior motivation, and it was this that had taken me by surprise, and caused me to turn from her without offering a light, which is what I might normally have done, had I not been subjected to such an imploring look. In an obscure way my failure to offer her a light appeared to me, rather than merely lacking in politeness, to have been an act of cowardice on my part. Perhaps the woman was afraid that I would turn her down (turn down, that is, the request for a smoke), but perhaps, and the idea grew in force the more I accommodated it, she wanted company, thought that I looked harmless, or was even attracted to me, and the plea for a cigarette was simply an opening gambit, which I might, if I had been someone else, or if I had been myself, under other circumstances (ie not with friends who were waiting for me just inside the museum's glass doors; not in a mood to endure the burden of another's sadness; not already spoken for, as they used to say, etc; there are so many conditions and disclaimers in any encounter of this kind), I might have asked her if she wished to take a drink, if it would not inconvenience her to join me for a coffee or a glass of wine; I would have posed my question in the most formal French I could muster, because, I must admit it, she was not unattractive and had an interesting look about her (if you discounted the wounded thing, which, after all, is pretty much a universal ploy). And as I mused over this possibility it struck me with absolute certainty that had my circumstances been different, if, beyond offering her a cigarette (step one), I had given her a light (step two) and then offered to take her for a drink (step three), we would, almost without doubt, have ended up in bed together. It was this premonition, this certitude, that had caused me to turn without offering her a light. Which left me wondering whether she was, in fact a prostitute, or simply a lonely woman in need of company, or of physical intimacy. And why should this bother me? I can't say it really did – and yet I turned away smartly, didn't offer her a light, could feel her eyes on my back – what it awoke in me was the realisation that one of those moments had passed, one of those so-called sliding-doors moments, and that this opening up of possibilities, this glimpse into a totally unexpected sequence of events set off an interior monologue, and although I had no desire to chat with or go to bed with this woman, I liked unravelling the likely play of events that would have ensued after offering her a light. I don't mean I fantasised about having sex with her; what interested me were the multiple ways in which we might both evade declaring outright what our intentions were, in order to carry out the almost mechanistic ritual of courtship, however hurried, since, unless she was actually on the game, some degree of social interaction would be necessary before we exchanged body fluids, or perhaps not; perhaps (and this hasn't happened to me for some years, and will almost certainly never happen to me again) she would have said I don't want a coffee or a glass of wine, Monsieur, please cut the small talk (small talk which, I'll be the first to admit, I am not very good at anyway), we both know where this is going, Monsieur, let's just go somewhere and *do it*. What interests me is the way these things develop, out of nothing, out of a glance, a stare, or the request for a cigarette, or more commonly, for a light. One consequence of the smoking ban is that such encounters no longer take place in warm, convivial public spaces. If the ban were to become total, a whole spectrum of social and sexual manoeuvring would be obliterated at a stroke.

I find the following in my notebook from April 1988, describing a Japanese girl whom I watched as she brushed her hair outside a café in Motril, near Granada.

It was as if she had to inspect each and every strand of her hair, knowing all along that she had no split ends, and then smoothing back the top of her head with the palm of her hand. Then she started looking at her arms, inspecting in detail her hands, her wrists, even rolling up her short sleeves and twisting her head (but gracefully, slowly) to inspect her shoulder as if expecting to find some alien shrub had implanted itself and bloomed there without her noticing. I could not yet see her face − approaching from behind I could only see the face of her companion, another Japanese − but there was a strange and formidable magnetism about her physical presence and I had to take a seat on the wall and I studied her face and it had all the contours and subtle depressions of an indolent beauty, restless eyes, a sorrowful mouth, and then as she watched me watching her she started again to brush her hair, so slowly and precisely, never taking her eyes off me. Like a cat washing herself, I thought, and while it would be understandable if she became self-conscious under the gaze of a stranger's eyes, it was clear by her actions that she actually relished the role of the observed since it gave her the power to return the gaze and become the observer. It was a relief when they paid and got up to leave and walked, very slowly, away.

In a sense, perhaps, the potential for an unfulfilled spontaneous erotic encounter is more interesting than those that *are* fulfilled, since the capacity for luxurious and solitary rumination is limitless, whereas the sudden eruption of a mutually experienced moment of lust evaporates with the question of what to do afterwards and the tedium of the predictable. What became of the French girl with whom I never spoke, one evening outside the cathedral of Bayonne, chatting with her friends beside the fountain in the square? She kept staring at me with those prolonged and erotically-charged gazes, with the nonchalant delivery that French women do so expertly. I was sitting on a bench near the cathedral door. I had no money and nothing to say to her, though I was, I suppose, flattered by the attention. Eventually the impotence of the situation got to me, nothing could ever come of this, I was a vagabond, a tramp. Not that this was obvious on this particular day, I must have recently acquired a new set of second-hand clothes from *Secours Catholique*, otherwise I daresay she would not have noticed me. Beggars and street-dwellers become invisible as objects of erotic charm to normal citizens, and apart from meetings with the occasional *vagabunda*, such as Charo, there were few opportunities for intimacy on the road.

I made my way into the cathedral, for something to do. It was dark and incense drifted across from a small side-chapel where a service was in progress, a dozen or so people gathered there, mostly old women, and the responses, the *ave marias* hauntingly sad; I remember wanting to weep, not for any reason, not even for self-pity, but simply because of the dark church and the singing and the incense and the hundreds of years of human prayer that occupied the building, breathed within it, an incubus of silent prayer that spread along the aisles and high towards the vaulted arches above me, a million silent or whispered prayers, whether or not they were answered, whether or not the people who made those prayers, the thousands of the faithful, now dead, had received any reward whatsoever for their efforts. I sat in the cathedral and listened to the remainder of the service, I enjoyed that, even enjoyed it when the old folks lined up to receive communion, but I was thinking, I cannot for a moment believe in the transubstantiation of the flesh into bread and wine, no not even wine, not for this so-called God of Love.

Outside, the girl and her friends had gone. A young man walked past me, then turned, and offered me ten francs to get something to eat. A miracle, I thought. God is Good.

This all seems such a long time ago.

They say that every cell in the body dies and is replaced at seven-year intervals; in this sense, I suppose, I am entirely distinct from the young vagabond who sat outside the cathedral at Bayonne, three times over. Whether or not this is literally the case, it sometimes feels, writing of those years, that I am observing the movements of an actor on a video that has become worn with age, and which flickers and shudders and occasionally blacks out altogether. "To write," says Maurice Blanchot, "is to pass from the first to the third person, so that what happens to me happens to no one, is anonymous insofar as it concerns me, repeats itself in an infinite dispersal."

And in this extended exercise of recollection (of the *I* that resembles a *he*), I begin to wonder why certain particular incidents come to mind rather than countless others which could equally well have served to illustrate those confounding years? I have not set out purposefully to sift through and select particular occasions or incidents, plotted something to make a coherent whole; on the contrary I have been led almost by instinct through a round of anecdotes and memories that have come to mind spontaneously through the process of writing itself. It is only by writing it that any sense of personal history has emerged.

Walter Benjamin writes that there is an angel who remembers the whole of history. His face is turned towards the past. He would like to pause and piece together everything that was smashed in the ongoing catastrophe of human affairs but there is a wind blowing from paradise and it is so strong that it gets caught up in his wings and he can no longer close them. The storm (which we call progress) drives him helplessly into the future, to which his back is turned, while the pile of rubble grows higher and higher.

It seems to me our personal histories are also formed this way; our consciousness of being in the world is an amalgam of debris swept together in the storm. Sometimes random objects – boxes, jewellery, pencils, pins, sticky tape, pieces of string, old coins – get caught up in the rubble and confuse the process of recollection. Fragments of other people's history, detritus from other minds and other worlds, errant particles, floating songs and poems, all make their way into the vaults of memory.

26

While the encephalopathy is a recent development and the insomnia has been an issue for around six years now, it is only in the past year or so that I have begun to feel, and look, like a sick man. Shortly after the hepatitis C was first diagnosed, back in 2000, it was suggested to me that I begin a course of treatment. Since the only drug therapy available for hepatitis C is a drug called Interferon (which was originally developed for the treatment of multiple sclerosis), I was asked if I would take part in a clinical trial for the drug, to be taken with Ribavirin, an anti-viral medicine. I was working full time, so elected to start the treatment in June, when the university would be settling into the summer recess. I was told that the success rate for patients with my strand or genotype of the virus stood at around 30-40%, although these statistics were probably optimistic.

Shortly after being diagnosed with hep C, and aware that there would be a wait before I commenced treatment, I went to see a Chinese herbal therapist in London, who came highly recommended, and with whom I have continued to visit – to the muted consternation of some, but not all, of my doctors – for the prescription of herbs and acupuncture. However, I stopped taking Chinese herbs when I started the Interferon treatment.

I administered the drugs myself, by subcutaneous injection, twice a week. The first injection brought on acute flu-like symptoms and I endured five or six hours of sweats, fever, nausea and dizziness. Mouth blisters, sore throat, headache, nosebleeds and nausea persisted for the first three weeks of the trial, but all told the symptoms were not as thoroughly debilitating as I had been led to expect, and after the third week I experienced hardly any side effects at all. However, the medication caused a decline in the manufacture of white blood cells (which constitute the body's immune system), and my platelet count dropped dangerously low. Platelets allow the blood to clot, so if I were to cut myself, for example, there was a danger I might bleed to death. My body felt shattered and I was mentally exhausted by the treatment. I returned to the Chinese herbal practitioner, received acupuncture and a new prescription of herbs. My general wellbeing and overall state of health improved immeasurably within a few days.

I was left disenchanted with the treatment I had received, and with the interpersonal skills of those administering the clinical trial. I know now what a difference it makes receiving treatment by caring, informed professionals. It didn't feel as though that was always the case during the clinical trial. Fortunately a new consultant hepatologist was appointed at my local hospital around this time and the quality of my care increased significantly, but it was considered too risky to put me back on Interferon treatment, and at the end of the summer I encountered a new setback. It was September, and I was, ironically, going over the details of a workshop I was planning to give in Cambridge for the British Medical Association with Glyn Elwyn, a senior researcher at the university, with whom I had written a number of papers on issues relating to decision-making during medical consultations, and the ways that doctors might be able to 'unpack' patient narratives. Glyn glanced at me once or twice during the course of our meeting, and asked if I was feeling all right. I wasn't – I'd been feeling under the weather for several days – but since this was par for the course with hepatitis C, I hadn't thought too much of it. Glyn, however, was concerned enough to call my hepatologist directly, and I was told to come along to the hospital right away. It transpired that I was bleeding internally from burst varices in the oesophagal passage, and was required to stay in hospital. Oesophagal bleeding can be extremely dangerous, and I was treated by gastroscopy, a lowering down the throat of a long bendy tube and miniature camera, which inspects the varices in the gullet. These are then 'bound', that is, the split ends of the varices are sealed back in place *in situ* by a skilled practitioner. Since this first happened, I have needed to have this carried out regularly, for the past five-and-a-half years.

I am not sure whether the Interferon treatment contributed directly to a decline in my health, but it felt as though this were the case at the time. Certainly the beta-blockers, with which I was treated in an attempt to address the oesophagal varices, with disastrous effects (dizziness, nausea, impotence) did me no good at all. However, any return to a potent drug therapy is now hypothetical, since there is no way that my liver would tolerate such powerful medication. I have continued visiting the Chinese herbalist and having acupuncture, which seems to help, temporarily, even if only by allowing me to sleep while the needles are in place, but I am fully aware that all attempts to treat my medical problems, other than a transplant, are provisional.

27

I have had to stop driving, except in emergencies. I have a tendency to drop off when waiting at traffic-lights, and longer journeys are a nightmare of enforced concentration, gripping the wheel with manic intensity, stretching and flexing my arms and legs, singing out loud, making up ludicrous songs in order to keep awake, although obviously I try to avoid this practice when there are other people in the car. Extraordinary how the insomniac will be overcome by sleep in the most inappropriate settings, but never, or hardly ever, when it is timely, at bedtime for example (how can I begin to describe the effect on me of an innocent phrase like 'bedtime', with all its cosy and infantile connotations of hot-water bottles and teddy bears, with its imposition of a well-rehearsed and ordered normality, or my envy on overhearing a comment such as "Oh, it's well past his bedtime", as though there was, or ever had been, a time designated specifically for bed, and slumber: in fact I think, my bitter, mirthful response to the expression conceals a tragic nostalgia for a time when bed-time meant something good).

There is no bedtime for the insomniac: you have given up deciding when you should sleep; instead, sleep decides when to take you, often at inopportune moments. In this sense, of course, any time is bed-time for the insomniac. I have even fallen asleep while giving a lecture, standing, like a horse, and although it was only for the briefest moment, and I don't think (but cannot be sure) that any of the students noticed, or if they did, were kind enough to let it pass, I can only imagine the look on my face when I started from my momentary slumber, looked up in astonishment and fumbled with my notes; poor fool, they must have thought, he's losing it, he probably doesn't know what day it is, he probably doesn't know his own name.

An insomniac is never short of advice from well-meaning friends and relatives. Everyone has experienced difficulty in getting to sleep, and many people feel that this qualifies them to offer advice based on the authority of experience. "Oh, I have trouble sleeping", they will tell you, and what they mean is that they have struggled from time to time to get to sleep, have tossed and turned for a while, or woken in the night and found it hard to return to their slumber; but essentially these setbacks rarely make a dent on their seven or eight hours of regular sleep. Such people find it impossible to conceive of the extent of disability endured by a serious Contender for the World Title, such as myself. Let me make it clear that insomnia is not a question of simply not being able to get to sleep – it is, cumulatively, a massive derangement of the senses, a perpendicular longing, a lacuna within narrative time, a backsliding acceleration into the entrails of night, awaiting the dawn as a mortally injured man might await morphine, in the hope that with the light will come sleep, if only for an hour, or half an hour.

One piece of sound advice from sleep counsellors is to impose a routine on your bed-time habits. Go to bed at a regular time, let's say eleven o'clock, eat carbohydrates an hour or so beforehand (I would favour porridge oats, which have calming properties), bathe my feet in buckets of alternating hot and cold water, five minutes of each, to combat RLS (Restless Legs Syndrome), meditate or practise some relaxing technique such as Qi Gong, take a sleeping potion, either prescription drugs or a strong compound of valerian, play a soothing tape (my favourite one is of waves breaking gently on a sea shore) and lay my head upon the pillow. And yes, I sometimes drop off for twenty minutes or half an hour, if I am lucky. And then I wake with a start, under the temporary illusion that I am utterly refreshed, as if I have slept for eight hours, and I reach for the alarm clock on my bedside table, swear or sigh, turn over, but immediately I know there is little point in even trying: my body has been invaded by several dozen small electric eels, swimming through the channels of my blood, causing me to twitch and jerk, especially the legs, the arms, and worst of all, this strange sensation of a charge being driven about, wildly, beneath the level of the flesh, like a cattle prod. *It's the virus,* I think, *the virus is taking over, dancing the viral dance*, it knows I am trying to rest, now is its chance to take over completely, and I twist and turn for a while, even take another pill, though not always, I know they have little effect and in any case are not helping the liver, not that that makes a lot of difference, the liver is shot, but I think those pills, diazepam, temazepam, nitrazepam, dalmane, zopiclone, do add to my general state of disorientation and confusion, and now I have stopped using them altogether; just as helpful to drink a herbal tea as swallow three temazepam, just as ineffective.

I have tried to persevere with the bedtime routine, even when it is so clearly not working, simply because I have run out of other ideas. But lately another element has crept into the equation: dread. I have begun to dread and even fear the allotted hour for slumber. It is not a dramatic sense of terror, more an apprehension that grows with the certainty of failure, borne out by the experience of a thousand sleepless nights. When this dread seeps into the mind and flesh, it becomes impossible even to consider the bedtime routine because the body resists all efforts to relax, to go with the flow, to become at peace with oneself, so essential to the process of sleep, and the restlessness in the limbs then becomes violent and vindictive, as though one's legs and arms have taken on a life of their own and will broach no compromise with sleep. In the early days of my illness, I would take myself for a run in the park, or a late-night swim at the health club, but with the oedema in my legs, these options are no longer possible. The dread of sleeping is exacerbated by a fear of waking with cramps. These have got steadily worse over the past year. At first they were regular cramps in the calf muscles, but more recently have begun to strike in the feet, and most painfully, the thighs. These thigh cramps are the worst, an agonizing rigidity sets in along the length of the thigh and up into the groin, causing a sudden paralysis: I wake screaming, an animal yelp that starts in the recesses of sleep and surges into wakefulness, attempt to massage the area vigorously, but almost always, as soon as I begin, the cramps will afflict the other leg, simultaneously, or the same leg, in another place, usually the calf or the foot itself. It is impossible to turn the leg in such a way as to relieve the pain, since with the slightest movement the pain intensifies. Sometimes it helps to swing the legs over the edge of the bed and attempt to stand, while continuing to rub with one hand, but since the locus of pain shifts so rapidly, it is not always easy to sustain this rubbing, while simultaneously hobbling about on one leg and letting forth bloodcurdling complaint, so an assistant is required, as the legs will not be moved without a helping hand, and my dear Rose, who has never once complained at being awakened by my loud and blasphemous cries, will always come to the rescue, and apply herself energetically to the task of massaging my wayward limbs, but since the locus of pain shifts so rapidly, it is not always easy for her to know where to begin. "No," I will whimper, "not there, *lower, higher, to the right, down...*": instructions that would try the patience of a saint. It is humiliating to be so helpless and in such pain that one cries out in the darkness of one's own home at the dead of night. Anyone who has suffered from cramps knows how painful and debilitating they are, but to be attacked by multiple cramps across several zones is way beyond my pain threshold.

Waking in this fashion, night after night, often after only half an hour's sleep, I give up. For long spells, I have resolved not to go to bed at all, and that has worked, after a fashion; I usually drop off around first light. For a while, when still going in to work, I operated in this way. I would spend the night reading and writing in my study, dropping like a stone at sunrise, sleeping until eight or nine in the morning, then getting up and going to my office. But once the cramps have set in, this path too becomes impossible to sustain. Extra salt might help, but doesn't, and is in any case dangerous, considering my medical complications. The doctors have prescribed me quinine, but it has no effect.

28

I can claim a modest expertise in different aspects of the labour involved in the cultivation of the olive and the production of extra virgin oil, having worked in several villages over the course of three winters, in Crete and in Zakinthos. I have tended the groves, weeding around the base of the trees with a *zapa*, learned to cut back and prune the less productive branches, worked on the harvest as a picker and heaver of sacks, and done various jobs in factories where the oil is produced. I have even been a victim of a minor industrial injury, thanks to a single flying olive. One morning, in a village near Kastelli, I inadvertently contrived a bizarre accident: battering olives from the branches with a short stick, one of the small hard fruits hit me in the eyeball, smacking into the cornea, causing a sudden shock and a twinge, but nothing more, until later, when I began to experience sharp stabbing sensations in the side of the head, and that evening, walking in under the strip lighting of the *kafeneion*, my skull rattled with sudden and startling pain, and I knew something within the eye was damaged.

The next morning I made my excuses to the farmer, took the bus into Hania, walked to the hospital and visited ophthalmology, where I received attention from a talkative young eye-doctor, who told me that injuries caused by flying olives were not uncommon at that time of year, a sentence which has resonated with me ever since, a weird and random thing to say in absolutely any other context or situation, but which seemed imbued with a certain grace. He explained to me how the hard surface of the olive implodes on the shiny moist layer covering the cornea, thereby causing damage to the inner part of the eye, which would need to be protected from direct light for a while. When he had finished examining me, he gave me a patch to wear over the left eye, which I slipped on with a sense of bravado, as though the wearing of a black patch might furnish me with some of that piratical swagger so much in evidence among the Cretans.

On leaving the hospital I decided to drop in at *To Diporto* for something to eat, and there I bumped into Hubert Tsarko, who had just finished a job on the olives somewhere out towards Rethimnon. After eating, we wandered down to Café Costas where we discovered a note recently left on the communal message board by Peter Green, and I quote: *I foolishly lent Richard 2000 drachmae and have gone to look for work in Kissamos.* The note was ostensibly addressed to Hubert, and yet exposed for every bystander to see, and to acknowledge and appreciate that it was evidently due to the first action that the second had been made incumbent upon him. That is, if he, Peter, whom everyone knew to be in poor health, an asthmatic, a chronic alcoholic, a renowned weakling, had not through his generosity and selflessness loaned me those 2000 drachmas then he might not have been forced to test his delicate constitution by resorting to hapless manual labour, a last resort for him (a last resort for his employers also) but would instead be here with us now, the centre of conviviality as always in Costa's bustling café, digressing interminably on some pet fad or delirious obsession (and I knew all his little stories, intended to beguile passing strangers into acts of spontaneous generosity, thereby to earn his thirsty jester's fee; I had heard every one of them so many times before, those fragmented addenda to the sad footnote that was Peter's life, a man given to the study of footnotes). Why even prefix the statement about going to look for work in Kissamos with the one about his foolhardy loan, unless to draw attention to the nefarious suggestion that to loan me any significant sum of money – significant enough, at least, for Peter to have deemed it worthy of proclamation to the world at large – was an act of folly?

Laughing out loud (but inwardly seething) I ripped Peter's note from the board and stuffed it in my pocket as a memento of his public calumny, and Hubert and I headed back towards Kastelli, and the farm where I had sustained my injury. I was granted a few days' rest until my eye healed up.

Each morning at Stilos – precisely the location at which Cochrane and his Spanish Republicans were ordered to organise a rearguard action against the Germans – I was sent on a truck, along with the boss's two sons, to the neighbouring smallholdings to collect the harvest of olives for processing. It was an exhausting job, not solely on account of the volume of work involved (the sacks, which could weigh up to seventy kilos, often had to be humped from the farmhouses up narrow tracks to the waiting lorry, where they were weighed on unwieldy portable scales) but because of the hospitality offered us at every home we visited, where we were plied with quantities of food and *tsikoudia*, a home-distilled spirit. Many of the smallholdings lay in the remotest and most inaccessible places, and the farmers, and especially their wives or mothers, were amused that a foreigner was a member of the collection party, and made a great fuss of me. The olive harvest was the most important event in the agricultural year, and it would have been deemed a grave insult to refuse this refreshment, but I soon learned that unless one paced oneself, it was a superhuman task to continue working throughout the day. As I was never capable of pacing myself the consequences were immediately apparent. More than once my knees buckled as I struggled up a slippery mud-track, much to the amusement of my companions, who, being Cretan males, regarded all non-Cretans – including other Greeks – as feeble and unmanly. We would work long after nightfall, returning to the factory, the truck laden with bulging sacks of olives, which had then to be unloaded, weighed again, and sorted for processing.

Since the full mechanisation of the process of oil production had not yet reached the smaller depots such as Stilos, the system employed was messy and back-breaking. The sacks of olives would be emptied into a vault and gobbled up by the oil-making machine. Layer upon layer of sticky copra mats, each with a hole in its centre, were piled onto a removable steel cylinder that formed the centrepiece of a large mobile trolley, and once this contraption had been manhandled into position beneath the huge hydraulic press, one could take a break until the pressing was completed, a procedure which took long enough to smoke a cigarette. Then the trolley was pulled away, and one by one the copra mats removed, each covered with the steaming residue of olives, a warm vegetable mash, waste material referred to generically as *skata*, or shit, which would be flicked off each mat with a single rapid movement, the clean mats being piled on the cylinder once more for the next round. Among the few foreigners employed there other than myself and Cacho, my South American housemate, I remember

Lorenzo, an anarchist from Barcelona, a man of prodigious physical strength and extreme goodwill in all respects excepting matters of religion. On the feast of Epiphany, the village priest visited the factory in order to bless the workers, to scatter holy water on us, and, with great solemnity, over the machinery, a rite that I found charming, indicating an animistic faith in the properties of objects, but one that incensed Lorenzo. The priest, excited into an excess of religious zeal by Lorenzo's atheistic protests, accelerated his movements, casting holy water over olive sacks, copra mats and, particularly, Lorenzo, soaking him. Only the hilarity of us onlookers, Greeks and foreigners alike, prevented the two of them from coming to blows.

In the early 1980s some of the remoter villages of the White Mountains were still quite primitive. I remember staying in Orthouni, where I slept in a shack loaned to me by the olive farmer. I was brushing my teeth one morning, standing by the door, and looked up to see an old woman pass by along the lane, riding side-saddle on a donkey, and I greeted her. She immediately began crossing herself, kicking her beast into a quick trot. That evening I learned from one of her relatives that the old lady had seen a strange man leering through the undergrowth and foaming at the mouth. She wondered if he had been bitten by a dog.

Working on the olive harvest itself, knocking the fruit from the trees with a stick, was always the most convivial of agricultural jobs. On a crisp winter's morning, scaling the larger trees with the help of ladders, you could gaze out over the steep orchards, the mountains rising sheer around you, sometimes catching a glimpse of the dark sea, far below. I remember one brilliant winter's day, after a fresh fall of snow, my improbable companion being a compatriot from Llanberis by the name of Jimmy Jones, an effusive nineteen-year-old whom I had met in the bars of Hania and invited back with me to the village of Orthouni. Eight hundred metres above sea level, Jimmy conversed with me in Welsh, in a tree, the snow unblemished on the slopes around us, here at the farthest edge of Europe.

After finishing the olive harvest, Hubert Tsarko and I set off for the Pelopponese, taking the ferry to Monemvassia, a place which I had long wanted to visit. Monemvassia was the home town of Yannis Ritsos, one of my favourite poets, although Ritsos himself was by then an old man, living in Athens. The town lies on an isthmus at the bottom end of the most easterly finger of the Peloponnese.

Ritsos is a poet of casual, almost offhand, but sublimely detailed observation. I had first discovered his work in the translations of Edmund Keeley, and later struggled through the original Greek, buying a handful of slim volumes from a bookseller in Iraklion. His writing was a revelation to me at the time, combining a crystalline compactness of narrative in the shorter poems with a corrosive sensuality, a startling awareness of the natural and inanimate world, imbued with the scents of the Greek landscape, the sounds of the sea, and an attention to the routine events of life. Ritsos spent a lifetime recording the details of things that lay in front of him, so that the most commonplace of scenes, a young woman resting her bicycle against a wall, a fisherman mending his nets, a spider crawling laboriously over the lip of a jug, the banging of a shutter against a wall at night, take on the qualities of enigma. The poems possess a ludic quality, along with this precise quality of observation, and while it remains a modernist and often surreal poetry, it nevertheless has as its recurrent reference point the storehouse of Greek myth.

There was not much remaining of the old town. I believe it has since been largely re-built, with the derelict medieval villas refurbished as holiday homes, but my abiding memory of that trip was of a walk through ghostly ruins in inclement weather, beneath the massive walls of the crusader castle, and of stopping off at a restaurant owned by relatives of Ritsos, with photographs of the town's most famous son adorning the walls of the small dining room. My hostess, a cousin or niece of the poet, had an elegant, patrician appearance, and she chatted with me amiably about the history of the town.

The Ritsos family history was as tragic as any Greek myth. At the start of the twentieth century, they were landowners of the upper-middle class, but the family fortunes were in decline, largely as a result of Yannis' father's obsessive gambling. The youngest of four children, Yannis lost his older brother, Dmitri, to tuberculosis, his mother dying from the same disease three months later. As an adolescent,

125

Yannis contracted TB himself, which would confine him to various sanatoria throughout his teens and twenties. At seventeen, his father was committed to an insane asylum at Daphni, near Athens. His sister, Loula, also suffered from mental illness and was institutionalized, indefinitely, in 1936.

I was the only customer, and the silence of the ruined town that surrounded us evoked a foreboding as ominous as the empty, haunted rooms of the old, decaying house of Ritsos' childhood, described in one of his most famous poems, 'The Moonlight Sonata', or of the thunderclouds that were gathering outside as we spoke long into the afternoon. When I left the restaurant, and headed down the narrow lane towards the isthmus, the clouds burst open, unleashing cold, fat drops of February rain that drenched me through. With the rain came thunder, and I strode from the deserted town like the sole survivor of a shipwreck, washed up on this inhospitable crusader shore, back to my hotel in the newer part of town, back to the mainland.

Hubert and I were soon out of funds, so we set off for the plains of Lakonia to look for work. We arrived, by chance as ever, in the village of Stefania, where we teamed up with Franco, an effusive Italian tenor from Trieste, and his diminutive, but impressively moustachioed Andalucian buddy, Antonio. There was an empty house in the village, which, we were told, had been left empty and unclaimed when its owner left for the USA thirty years before, and which we occupied until it became overcrowded; later, with the onset of spring and warmer weather, we set up camp near a stream that ran through a wooded valley a couple of kilometres from the village. The most memorable feature of Stefania was the preponderance of people with enormous ears: it must have been a genetic trait. We stuck around, since there was plenty of work on the oranges.

29

By May Hubert had moved on and most of the work available was confined to the *thermokypia*, large plastic hothouses where tomatoes were grown. The task of working long hours in the stifling heat, the stench of the plants, and the sticky residue of insecticide that stained clothing and skin, causing a rash that itched irredeemably, inspired an aversion to tomatoes from which I have never fully recovered. We would start early, in order to make the most of the cooler hours before midday, by which time the greenhouses reached temperatures of 50 degrees centigrade, making further labour impossible. I was working regularly for a farmer called Dmitri, who would come and seek me out for work even when others were available, perhaps because I spoke Greek.

One Sunday afternoon I was down by the stream with Franco, Antonio, an Israeli woman called Hannah and a few others. It was a secluded and magical place: small trees and fragrant azalea lined the banks of the stream and there was an abundance of unusual birdsong. Antonio had prepared a brew with the seeds of the datura plant, a powerful hallucinogen that grows wild in most areas of the Mediterranean, and about which I knew very little, apart from second-hand, through my readings of the fantasist Carlos Castaneda, whose works of suspect anthropology had once provided a welcome diversion from the plodding functionalism of Radcliffe-Brown and Evans-Pritchard or the structuralism of Claude Lévi-Strauss (I had, as a student, wondered whether a double-barrelled name was *de rigueur* for top-notch anthropologists: my tutor was an affable English aristocrat called Julian Pitt-Rivers).

Datura, also known as jimson weed or thorn-apple or devil's weed, is a dangerous sort of plant. Years later, in Spain, I came across a reference to it in an encyclopaedia of plants, and the entry was enigmatic. A translation might be ventured thus: "the plant grows freely in most areas, especially scrubland, backyards and at roadsides, and is easily found, *except by those who are specifically looking for it.*" This qualification seemed out of place in a reference book. Also in Spain, when I was staying at the Cabo de Gato, in a ruined village that had been colonised as a sort of hippy Shangri-la, a young German tourist had disappeared into the sea after allegedly being fed datura by his prankster girlfriend, stripping off and swimming out into oblivion.

Because it is picked in the wild, and the seeds either eaten or brewed as a tea, it is difficult to monitor dosage, and potency will vary according to many factors, including the maturity of the seeds when picked and the manner in which it is prepared. It is extremely powerful and can induce a severely toxic reaction. In terms of the hallucinogenic experience, datura is a world apart from LSD or mescaline: recreational it is not. It will, if such language has any meaning, attempt to infiltrate the soul. For days after drinking the brew I felt infused by an extraordinarily combustible energy, tinged with an acute sense of the fragility of my habitual perceptions of reality. Specifically, I was made acutely aware of the existence, parallel to our own visible world, of a wondrous and terrifying otherworld in which we were unwitting participants. That this other world was as real as the one we normally inhabit was never in doubt while under the influence of the datura plant. I still retain the vivid impression that for one night and a part of the following day the veil between these worlds had been removed.

When the effects of the potion made themselves felt, all three of us began to behave strangely, but none more so than Antonio, who trailed his sleeping bag into the stream and attempted to lie down in it. Franco and I pulled him out and tried to dry him off, but Antonio would have none of it, returning repeatedly to the stream with his sleeping bag and lying in the water. His movements resembled those of a character in a fairy tale who has been put under a spell. Eventually someone made a fire and we managed to lure Antonio away from the stream; he now appeared entranced by the fire. I remember hoping he did not attempt the same trick with his sleeping bag. My memory of this passage is relatively clear, but in the following hours, as darkness fell, things become a little confused. I have to rely mainly on the account given to me afterwards by Hannah, the Israeli, who stayed by my side throughout the night as my self-appointed minder. According to her, after helping to rescue Antonio from a watery grave, I took myself across the stream and sat on the ground near a large bush, and began talking at it. I kept up an animated conversation with the bush for several hours and appeared quite focused and unmuddled. Hannah could not understand much of what I was saying as I apparently spoke a mix of languages not within her repertoire. My own memory of the night is dominated by two figures in the bush. I have no idea who they were, and to this day continue to reflect on their nature. They were male, and were, like me, seated on the ground. Their faces resembled the mud masks worn by New Guinea shamans: long, white, almost featureless faces, rectangular in shape. They had no lips, only a shadowy gap from which their voices emanated, and similarly, black peepholes served as eyes. They sat cross-legged and were naked; their skin was daubed in the same thick white paint, or paste, as their faces. Often they spoke at the same time, and I seem to recall that they were saying different things, simultaneously, but that I was able to understand both with utmost clarity. I knew that they had come for me, but I was unwilling to let them take me. I knew, too, that I could not afford to respond with anything less than cool precision, that I must, above all, remain calm, indeed, that my life depended on it. The figures were not terrifying in any conventional sense, and they were not simple cardboard cut-outs but entirely three dimensional. If they had formally announced themselves as emissaries of death, I would not have been surprised. Although I cannot remember the words, nor even the precise context of our talk, I do have the strong impression that I was arguing for my life: that everything, but everything, depended on the outcome of this challenge. It probably does not matter that I have no idea what we said; more important was that I came through it and the sensations I bore with me when I returned. These were a compound of relief, intellectual exhaustion and a strangely vibrant awareness of my own spiritual (for want of a better word) potential, indeed of the endless potential for insights of a transcendental kind, once one had drawn aside the curtain separating our everyday existence and the other, normally invisible world that I discovered that night. I do remember feeling that, while they were messengers, envoys of some kind, from an unseen world, and potentially dangerous to me, they were by no means simply my enemies: they were, paradoxically, allied to me in some significant fashion. They might well, in psychological terms (to use an entirely different system of reference) be termed conflicting aspects of the psyche, but that does not really help, because by accepting any purely psychological explanation, by shifting to another paradigm, one that attempts to *explain* the events of my datura experience, I somehow lose sight of the thing in phenomenological terms – in terms of lived experience. I only have recourse to the events as I recall them. Those events can be termed hallucinations, but that does not help me understand them: they were real enough at the time.

The following morning I walked up to the village of Stefania with Franco and Antonio, both of them extremely fragile, whereas I felt buoyant and infused with a clairvoyant energy. I remember looking at my reflection in the bathroom mirror of the café and being startled by the clear whiteness of my eyes, which seemed to corroborate the precision and acuity of my vision. I was seeing things with an exaggerated clarity, and most of what I saw conveyed an intensely luminous quality. We sat on the terrace of the café and drank orange juice. Dmitri, the farmer for whom I regularly worked, came by on his tractor. He told me he needed some help with his tomatoes, two or three hours work at most. Franco and Antonio protested as I leaped up to join Dmitri on his tractor, riding shotgun on the tyre-guard.

The tomatoes were already picked and waiting in boxes along the aisles of the greenhouse. My job was to load them onto a trolley and deliver them, four or five boxes at a time, to the roadside, where they would be piled high, ready for the market lorry that would take them to Athens that night. It was already sweltering inside the greenhouse, since it was by now mid-morning. I was working alone. All I had to do was complete this task, and I would be able to return to the café and re-join my friends, or else borrow Dmitri's motorbike and ride down to the nearest beach, a few miles away, for a swim.

I stripped down to shorts and trainers and began collecting boxes from the far end of the greenhouse, working gradually back towards the entrance. Although I had not slept the previous night, I was not tired; on the contrary I had a surplus of energy and careered back and forth along the muddy pathways with the trolley perilously overladen, six crates at a time. Dmitri was working outside, in the shade of a tree, calmly sorting the tomatoes. He had offered me a price for the job, rather than pay by the hour, so there was no reason to hang about.

I was half way through the task when I noticed movement among plants further down the aisle on which I was working. It was a fleeting glimpse, nothing more, but on the next aisle I noticed it again, as I bent to lift a crate: a definite presence amongst the tomato plants. I stood straight and looked around, but continued with my work, piling the boxes onto the trolley, while keeping an eye on the plants furthest along the line. Then, like a character at a masked ball, one of the grotesque mud-men from the night before appeared at the end of the row, peering at me down the line of tomato plants: the same oblong face, glaringly, painfully white in the dense humidity of the hothouse, the same dark slits for eyes, the sad black hole of a gob.

I dropped the crate I was carrying, tomatoes spilling onto the ground at my feet. The figure – who was the size of a small adult – retreated, almost coyly, behind the row, and then re-appeared seconds later, a little closer to me, parting two tomato plants with its pale hands, and stared at me blankly. I was definitely alarmed, but was not going to take any nonsense. Let me clarify: it is possible to recognise the fact that one is hallucinating, but the capacity of the rational mind to distance itself from the object of one's hallucinatory gaze does not make it any easier to contend with. It is possible, in other words, to hallucinate and at the same time to know that one is hallucinating, if indeed, that was the case, for who can ever say, definitively and without reservation that a thing is real or not, when that reality is so configured as to confound or challenge our most basic and cherished presuppositions.

I spoke to it. It bent its oversized head to one side, like an attentive dog. I told it to go back to from whence it had come. It appeared to be listening, but made no response. I told it I had work to do, and unless it wanted to help me shift crates of tomatoes, make itself useful, it had best be on its way. I had to re-assert the ascendancy of the Real World. I was Captain Sensible: it was the Unearthly Pook. I was No-Nonsense Joe: it was the Phantom of the Hothouse. It turned its face full towards me and emitted a curious whistling sound, low and tremulous. I was reluctant to approach: I was unsure what power it had over me, even if it were unreal, even if it were some weird projection from the abyss of my unconscious mind. I raised my voice, told it that I had enough complications in my life without adding to them any kind of intercourse with imaginary beings. Its face remained turned towards me: it did not speak, but continued to make this strange quavering whistle, like wind through reeds. And for a long, expectant moment we remained like that, I and it, and as I calmed down, the creature gradually ceased to be a threatening presence, and instead I felt its impenetrable sadness, its terrible lack, and I knew it could not harm me, I could only harm myself.

Dmitri appeared at the entrance to the greenhouse, thirty paces away, and called out to me. He had heard me shouting, he said, and wondered what was going on. Was anything wrong? There he stood, in marked contrast to my ghostly interlocutor, a very real and rather chubby Greek, with curly black hair, blue shorts and a striped tee shirt. No, I called back, everything was fine, I had been reciting poetry, I told him, loudly, the kind of answer that he would have expected from me. He laughed, shook his head, and waddled out again. When I turned back to look at mud-man, there was no trace of him. I set off and searched up and down the rows of plants, but could not find him. Eventually, when Dmitri called out for more crates, I gave up looking.

30

I have two recordings of Glenn Gould playing Bach's Goldberg Variations on the piano. The first was made in 1955, the year before I was born, and the second in 1981, shortly before the pianist's death, the same year that I left London and went to live in Crete. The second version is quite different from the first, and lasts several minutes longer. I think of the earlier recording as a day-time piece, and the second as nocturnal. They are both sublime, but in the first Gould is the young concert pianist on a mission, and he dazzles with his technical brilliance, his impeccable sense of timing. By the time he made the later recording he had nothing to prove, he had achieved everything a virtuoso pianist might reasonably be expected to achieve and more, and while there is no trace of complacency to the playing, it exudes a certain detached or entranced quality. Possibly the second version is more exacting, more profound, he lingers over the notes of the first variation with a confidence that is not to be confused with arrogance, a confidence that conveys a total acquaintance with, and mastery of, the music, a familiarity with every phrase, every musical innuendo, the fruit of years of study, and he is able to hover, and to hoist the listener into a space above and beyond the music, to linger there in a state of wonder, a phrase the pianist himself made use of. The album notes carry a quote from Gould: "The purpose of art is not the release of a momentary ejection of adrenalin but rather the gradual, lifelong construction of a state of wonder and serenity."

There are two photographs of the artist, taken in the respective years the recordings were made. In the first he is young, quite handsome even, or dashing, his hair flopping over his eyes, while in the later photo his hair has thinned and he is wearing glasses. In both pictures his concentration is almost palpable, and in both his mouth is open, not significantly, not gawping, but open, as though he was concentrating so hard that he had forgotten to close it, or had opened it to say something, and forgotten his lines – or to groan (his recordings are marked by these occasional groans, which should be disturbing, but are not).

Glenn Gould's recordings of Bach keep me company for long hours, while I sit at my desk. He is a faultless companion, especially when I am struggling to impose order on my thoughts. I would like to catch some of the fallout from his playing, inform my own thought with some of that rigour, that clarity of intent, employ his music as a force-field against the fatigue that overtakes me as I type away, as a weapon against the viral dance, against the affliction of sleeplessness, in an inverse sense to the one in which they were first intended: for, ironically, Bach is supposed to have written the Goldberg Variations around 1741 to ease the nocturnal insomnia of his patron, Count Keyserling.

The insomniac becomes obsessed with the minutiae of time, the details of its measurement. The insomniac is the acolyte of time, its devotee and its principal blasphemer. When I listen to Glenn Gould's two recordings of the Goldberg Variations, I recognise a fellow obsessive over these questions of the minutiae of time, and its measurement, and I suspect, or rather have decided, that Gould was probably an insomniac, or if he wasn't he should have been. But I know for certain he was obsessed with timing his performances.

For the past couple of weeks I have been noting down the number of hours that I spend sleeping. Including the random and unplanned naps that I have mentioned, I have discovered that my average daily consumption of sleep is around two hours. Obviously since that is an average, there are days (or nights) when I will sleep more, and nights (or days) when I sleep less. If I manage to get three hours in one uninterrupted session I wake up with the gratification of a small triumph, as though I had gorged myself on sleep, outwitting the phantoms of sleeplessness, who plot against me, and I imagine to be my enemies. I know I am deranged, but the ghosts are real. I conceive of them physically, and they take the form of the white-masked mud-men I met in the bush near Stefania. They plan to suck my breath from me, and to leave me famished of sleep. One spectacular night, last November, after a tormented few days of no sleep at all, I slept eight hours through, a miracle, and woke with a sense of panic, as though by sleeping for so long I had missed something essential; what precisely, I could not have said, but the closest I can get to an explanation for my panic, or guilt, would be this: *that I had slept while the other me, the insomniac me, had suffered the night in terrible solitude, and that I (who had been asleep) should have been keeping him (i.e. myself) company.*

I believe this is called the disintegration of the self. It is the same condition that had me thinking I could phone myself at the book launch and it seems to be an endemic part of my illness. If it continues I suppose I should request psychiatric help, but as far as I am concerned, this fragmentation of my personality, while deviant to any onlooker, makes perfect sense. The aspects of the self that had previously cohered in one person are taking on a life of their own.

There is no way for me to rationalise my thoughts about sleep, or the lack of it. Everything becomes measurable only in terms of hours and minutes. I have calculated, on the basis of experience, that I need five hours sleep to function reasonably, on a continual basis. I can, as they say, get by quite happily on five (though I would be happier still with six). Seven or eight hours would be very nice but I have to be realistic. I have never been one of those people who needs his eight hours, or else is left grumpy and disconsolate throughout the day. My body, I feel, needs five. And it is getting, on average, about two. Things are beginning to fall apart. My brain is not functioning as it should. It hurts me to think. I earn my living principally by thinking, and it hurts me to think. That cannot be good.

My GP has put my name down to attend a sleep clinic near Cambridge, but I am unlikely to be accepted there while awaiting a liver transplant, and who knows, if I receive a successful transplant, my sleep patterns might re-adjust. Professor E, at Birmingham, has advised me that my insomnia will not necessarily be cured with possession of a new liver, but I choose to hope otherwise. I cannot bear to imagine an interminable future blighted by sleep deprivation. I fantasize about sleep. I even gain a vicarious satisfaction by watching others sleep. I have crept into my daughters' rooms at night and sat at the edge of their beds, each in turn, watched the sweet serenity that sleep bestows upon their faces. I am not envious of them, I do not wish to disturb them, and I swallow the scene down in great draughts. The sight of them, relaxed in gentle slumber, is almost more than I can bear. I feel swamped by love, by an almighty onrush of protective love. I leave quietly and climb the stairs back to the loft.

31

I have just finished reading a collection of stories by Roberto Bolaño. They leave me with a strange sensation, as though I had read them before and were simply re-reading, or as if the things that were being described had happened to me personally, in a distantly remembered life. The cover blurb informs me that Bolaño died in 2003, at the age of fifty, while awaiting a liver transplant. I know this already, but as a man of fifty myself, waiting for a liver transplant, the sentence still has a particular resonance. Bolaño, like me, was a writer prone to reckless travel and troubled by a history of substance abuse; like me, he had lived in Barcelona, and worked extensively in lowly jobs around the Mediterranean. We both eventually wound up in the north-eastern corner of Spain, in the province of Girona; he at Blanes, myself a little inland and further north, at Rabós.

I met Bolaño while grape-picking in the south-west of France, when we were quite young. Or rather, I have a memory of sitting in a bar, reading a collection of short stories by William Burroughs and this guy taking a seat opposite me, and I remember discussing Burroughs with the person who may or may not have been Bolaño, who talked incessantly, in Spanish – a language in which I was by no means fluent at the time – interspersed with passages of bad French when I displayed my lack of understanding. He seemed to have an intense grasp of world literature, had the wild range and anarchic confidence of the autodidact, which I recognised, and he seemed to really like talking, enjoyed the chase of ideas and wordplay and of any insane incongruence that came along. Afterwards we got pretty drunk and Roberto ranted about a passport and I can recall sitting in a small park where we exchanged extravagant insults with a pack of feral Romani kids.

Three decades on, I was sitting in a New York hotel room and I saw his picture in a magazine, and immediately recognised him, though his hair was shorter in the photograph. He had been dead for five years.

But was it Bolaño I met? I definitely remember meeting a Chilean who, in my memory, resembles the man in the photo, with whom I spent a night drinking in the town of Lézignan-Corbières, and that should be enough, but I am also aware that memory can be an unreliable accomplice. As if to confirm, and then again, to deny, that unreliability, I receive an unexpected phone call from Hubert Tsarko, the only known survivor, apart from myself, of that group of vagabonds from the 1980s, who is – for reasons I find difficult to fathom – in Liverpool. He normally lives in Athens, or on various Greek islands, where he makes a living as an itinerant bouzouki player. I ask him about Bolaño.

"A Chilean?" he repeats after me, "thin guy, curly hair, round glasses? Possible. No, I've not heard of him. Roberto? No idea. I don't remember any writers, but you wouldn't necessarily divulge that kind of thing, would you? It's like, you know, a secret vice. Well, he might have to you, but I don't remember speaking with him. There was a group of Spanish there. Maybe there was a Chilean with them. You were with that girl, the *valenciana*, Alicia. You must remember her. It was around the time we got slung in the cells by the gendarmes."

This is all a blank, including my alleged association with a Valencian called Alicia, although Hubert's mention of the name does conjure a blurry, pleasing vision: but is that a true memory or am I inventing her, responding to his remark in the same way we might fill in the blank with the first word that comes to mind when presented with an impossible cloze test, or painting by numbers when the numbers have not been allocated colours? If I can't properly remember Alicia, with whom I was presumably enjoying carnal relations – the insinuation of 'you must remember her' left little doubt – how come I can remember Roberto? Have I made this up?

In the last of Bolaño's stories in *Last Evenings on Earth*, called 'Dance Card', one of the characters mentions that the great Chilean poet Nicanor Parra once stayed at his house, and the narrator comments: "In this statement I glimpsed a childlike pride which I have noticed again and again in the majority of writers". Is my insistence that I recognise the face of Bolaño something similar, a wish to be associated with the author, one which nobody can now disprove? I doubt it. I recognised him from the photograph before I had read any of his work or had any reason to wish to be associated with him, before I had discovered our literary or biographical kinship, even our shared medical condition as citizens from the same province in the kingdom of the sick.

"We were arrested? In Lézignan?"

"Oh yes. All because of some English cretin who tried to steal a car, practically in front of the gendarmerie. They hauled us all in, you, me, and the Englishman – not the Spanish, they weren't with us then – and locked us up for a few hours, then kicked us out, told us to leave town."

"I can't remember any of this. Tell me more."

"Alberto and company. Milou?"

"Come again?"

"You don't remember the Brazilians? You don't remember the little white dog that slept outside the patisserie?"

"None of it. Perhaps I only remember the things I want to remember."

"No, that is certainly not the case. You would remember Alicia if that were true. Do you remember the fighting Serbs? Or the *wolf hombre*? How about the moon in the stadium? Do you remember Peter's poem about the moon in the stadium being blue?"

"That was Riscle, not Lézignan. I always thought the blue moon thing was in Riscle. And the fighting Serbs, weren't they in... *Serbia?* Hubert, none of this makes sense. I don't know whether it's my illness doing this or normal memory loss. As for the *wolf hombre* – help me out here Hubert, *who was the* wolf hombre?"

"The *wolf hombre* descended on us in Stefania, when we were living in the house with the broken door and graffiti on the bedroom wall that went: *why for you make me angry when you sleep like tractor machine?* He was a Swiss physics graduate, keen to tackle the big ontological questions. You had very little patience with him. When he left us, Luz – you must remember Luz, from Santander – well, she came out with the immortal line, *el wolf hombre est parti.* However, before the *wolf hombre* left, he explained Schrödinger's cat to me."

Hubert pauses for a moment, as though the process of remembering had created a hiatus in the act of telling.

"What amuses me now is that among all the things you cannot

remember there are some real gems. Do you remember the replies you routinely gave to people when they asked how you lost your fingers?"

"Oh God, no. Please Hubert, spare me." The phantom of recurrent drunken fabulation hovers before me, even after so many years of abstinence.

"Well, first time round, you were, let's see, a freedom fighter in Eritrea. A convincing tale. You evoked the bleak mountain landscape, the scorching sun, dust. Oh, the dust, Richard, you were good on dust, strong on dust and heat and thirst. You evoked the dryness of the throat with such efficacy that your listeners would become thirsty themselves and feel obliged to buy you a drink. Kalashnikov slung over your bloody shoulder. Ambushed by Ethiopian forces, the machine gun ra-tat-tat-tat, being stretchered by your loyal comrades-in-arms to a makeshift bush hospital. A latter day Rimbaud, with a conscience, fighting for a cause. That one would get admiring glances. The women liked that one. Then there was the fall-back story, of how you lost your fingers dynamiting fish. That one didn't go down quite so well in Greece, of course; too many Greeks with their own digits missing after lobbing a few sticks of high explosive into the Aegean."

Hubert pauses again, waiting for my response, but none is forthcoming. He is, perhaps, as surprised that I have gone vacant on the war in Eritrea, dynamiting fish, Brazilians, the little white dog, the blue moon and the *wolf hombre*, as I am that he can remember all these details, or at least some of them – and they all nag at me, spectres of a life long left behind – but not the one that interests me most, concerning Roberto Bolaño. Perhaps my memory of meeting him is some kind of aberration; but really, why should I care to invent such a meeting? And the photograph is definitely familiar. Yet still I hesitate: while there are extended tracts from the decade of my twenties that are retained with crystal clarity, the three consecutive grape-picking autumns of '83 to '85 have lost all definition. I was, to be fair, at the peak of my dishevelment over this period.

"What years were we in Lézignan, Hubert?"

"Oh I don't know. Sometime in the eighties."

I dwell in the (possibly false) memory for a while. But later, when

I have put the phone down and returned to my desk, it suddenly dawns on me: I am getting my chronology all wrong. My alleged meeting with Bolaño was not in the eighties after all, it must have been 1979, when I escaped from London for a spell of grape picking, to get away from both Natasha and my job, before I even met Hubert Tsarko, and the past is now a wounded animal slipping away from me at nightfall, sneaking into the forest, and I have left off thinking about the confabulations of memory and of what might or might not have happened. It is evening in the little park at Lézignan near the *Maison des Jeunes* and I am sitting on a bench. The sky is a deep violet. Roberto is there, kicking a football around with the gypsy kids. For a moment the image is complete, has the unmistakeable texture of reality: then it is gone.

32

Natasha died from a heroin overdose one night in September 1988, a week before her thirty-fifth birthday. I received the news in a phone call from her sister, while doing rehab at a very strange clinic in the Pyrenees. Natasha's body was held for a long time following the autopsy, as there were suspicious circumstances surrounding her death. Her Aunt Viola, who had flown over to London, dissuaded me from going there myself, since, she said, I was doing well and she did not want me getting upset and relapsing or, who knows, seeking some kind of revenge. Natasha had been living with a twenty-year-old junkie, and her family were trying to get him to take some responsibility for what had happened and he was doing his best to avoid them. Natasha was not a regular user, and the boyfriend was clearly responsible for the tragedy, which was due to the unusual purity of the drug. It all sounded grim. During my years of wandering, I had never entirely lost contact with Natasha. She had been over to visit me when I stayed with her family in Florence, and again in Crete. We had met up once in Belgium. We never fully let go, and the news was hard to bear.

Tavertet, high in the mountains above the town of Vic, offered a breezy sanctuary from the summer heat that seared the plains below. It is a dramatic location: the village itself, a collection of thirty or so houses, stands on a promontory of elevated land, sheer cliffs falling on three sides. A thousand metres below, beyond thick forest, lies the reservoir of Sau, from whose waters, depending on the season, is visible the spire of the drowned village church. That summer the water was so low that not only the spire, but the supporting structure and the roofs of other buildings were to be seen protruding from the man-made lake. I tried to imagine how it might feel for any survivors of the village of Sau, standing there from the vantage point of Tavertet, and seeing the intelligible remains of their homes, drowned forever.

In spite of the dramatic location, Tavertet was a soulless place. Most of the original properties had been renovated as holiday homes for visitors from Barcelona, and there seemed to be some kind of contest as to who could maintain the greenest lawn, the most picturesque of little gardens (this in a village where water was scarce and had to be brought in by tanker). The *Kensho* centre, which owned three houses and a small hotel and restaurant in the centre of the village, was regarded with suspicion by the locals, and not without reason. It imposed on its residents a regime centred on macrobiotic diet and phony Zen. Founded by a mysterious benefactor, whom I never met, it sought to provide a place of contemplation and retreat for a variety of gullible and neurotic guests, and fed them a stew of philosophical vagaries developed by the director, Juan Carlos, a guru type and ex-Olympic walker, who bore an unnerving resemblance to the English comic actor, Charles Hawtrey, of *Carry On* fame. Juan Carlos made quite stupendous claims for his healing powers, treating cancer patients and the mentally unwell alongside the addicts who formed his battery of kitchen staff and general labourers. I had been referred to the place after falling ill in Figueres. Since I had no money I was granted a place on the team in exchange for giving Juan Carlos English lessons.

Although I did not receive any helpful advice from Juan Carlos about changing fundamental patterns of behaviour – the only effective way to treat addictive illness – I did stop drinking. Juan Carlos, meanwhile, showed absolutely no ability as a student of English. In fact he was a hopeless case. While there, however, I began a relationship, rather unwisely in some regards, with one of the therapists, a hyper-charged young Catalan woman, and shortly afterwards I moved out of the *Kensho* centre. At first I stayed near Tavertet, where I earned my living as caretaker of a small castle in the Collsdecabra mountains, which was quite easily the best job I have ever had; but after a few months, I moved down to Barcelona after Montse, my erstwhile therapist, invited me to live at her place in Fabra i Puig. Our domestic arrangements were predicated on the basis that I drank no alcohol and I serviced her regularly and robustly, thus maintaining the elevated passion of our first few weeks together, when, to our mutual satisfaction, we spent much of our time, in Montse's preferred phrase, *follando como locos* – fucking like maniacs. Sober sex was a novel experience for me and I appreciated its therapeutic value.

In these happy domestic circumstances I found work freelancing as a researcher with a publishing house, and then – with a wholly fictional CV – teaching English at a school in the well-heeled Sarria district of the city. In addition I took on private students and began earning, at least by the standards to which I had become accustomed, very good money. These were the days of the TEFL boom in Spain. I had a glamorous Catalan girlfriend, I bought a car, took trips out of the city with Montse, and I made new friends: Catalans, Latinos, and a few of the Brits I met at work.

I continued to abstain from alcohol (which was not easy when socialising with the British) but my sobriety was shaky and I was hanging by a thread. I almost certainly transferred my compulsive behaviours elsewhere and ultimately failed to fulfil the full terms of my contract with Montse, in spite of her being a most attractive woman. When she and I parted company I found myself an attic flat in the Gothic quarter. A year later, when I finally picked up a drink, my fall from grace was immeasurably worse than on any previous occasion. I lost my job, wrote off the car, gave notice on my apartment and set off once again. My despair was real, but gilded with an indistinct sense of relief.

33

I travelled light, as usual, carrying a brown canvas satchel containing only a thin blanket, a toothbrush, a good pocketknife, notebook, pencils and a tattered edition of Cavafy, a poet once described by E.M. Forster as *standing absolutely motionless, at a slight angle to the universe.*

I took only one set of clothes: jeans, a shirt and sweater and – when I could find them – strong shoes, or else rope-soled espadrilles, discarding and replacing them at any convenient *secours catholique,* a service provided across France, which hands out food and clothing for vagabonds and the homeless. In Spain the same service was provided by an organisation called *caritas.* As a rule I walked, covering big distances in this way, but occasionally I jumped a train, or hitched a lift, depending on how sociable I was feeling, and how urgent my need to get to places.

A brutally cold night in the city of Burgos, too frozen even to consider looking for a place to lie down and court hypothermia, wandering the streets, hands deep in my pockets, collar turned up against the icy wind that cut through the thin cloth of my coat. I shared a beer with a young conscript from Santander serving his time in the military with profound resentment, who told me this is *una ciudad fascista,* a fascist city, but I remember neither arriving nor departing, only walking the streets in the numbing cold, in such a way, that is, that the lack of any memory of arrival or departure makes me question whether I was ever there at all, or if indeed I went there once, and died from some species of forlorn heroism, and therefore never left, and am a ghost perpetually circling the grandiose and idiotic statue of *El Cid.*

So many nights sleeping rough in vile locations, the nocturnal search for cardboard casing to be ripped open and spread beneath me, above me, attempting some fruitless attempt at insulation and cover. How to contrive a purpose in this endless pursuit of the basic requirements of warmth and shelter, sustenance and sleep? San Sebastian: *Plaza de la Trinidad* once again. Am I on some obstinate quest to find the lovely

Charo, last seen five years earlier, pursued by demons she could not name? I watch the tall junky with bad teeth scraping at the stonework of a sandstone wall with a nailfile, procuring a fine powder, which he will fold into wraps and sell to desperate addicts or to French tourists suffering from *nostalgie de la boue* as golden brown heroin. I am wondering whether to break the first rule of the street-dweller – live and let live – by walking over and pointing out to him the considerable error of his ways. I'm in the mood.

In Lugo, a Galician city founded by the Romans, I sleep in a derelict building along with other down-and-outs, and am awakened by a terrible stench. Relieved to discover I am not its source, but unable to return to sleep, I stumble down to street level in order to find something to relieve the delirium tremens. Down the cobbled lane, shivering with cold, the early sun filtering through the mist, I can hear a sound behind me. Glancing back, I see a man approaching. He is wearing a broad-rimmed hat and is whistling in a brassy, tuneless fashion. I continue on my way, entering the café in which I regularly buy wine. I have enough loose change for a single bottle, which the bartender fills from a huge wooden barrel in the shadows behind the bar. When he returns with my bottle, the *caballero* (who has followed me into the café) slaps down the payment for my wine, wishes me a good day, and orders for himself. He does not attempt to engage me in conversation or want anything in return.

I glance at the newspaper he has unfolded on the surface of the bar. It is 23rd September, the anniversary of Natasha's death. My pleasure at the stranger's act of spontaneous generosity is at once swamped by a gut-wrenching sense of loss. I go outside and sit on the steps facing the cathedral. A wind begins to blow up, dispelling the early morning mist, coursing noisily down the narrow lanes that converge on the cathedral square, and causing bystanders and pedestrians to clutch at their hats and bend their shoulders against its force. My attention is caught by a loose plastic bag, which is blown in spiralling circles up into the air and down again, dragged just above the surface of the paving stones to the walls of the great cathedral, then sucked up on a draught and travelling halfway across the square at a height of twenty or thirty feet, then, in a slow whirl of somersaults, tumbling and sinking like a deflated balloon, almost to ground level, before being caught on a fresh gust and hoisted skyward once more. I watch the bag with fascination, tinged with a sense of horror, and remember Natasha. As always happens, whenever I reconstruct the circumstances of her death, I begin to wonder if there was any way, in spite of being in another country at the time, in spite of our having been separated for so long, in which I could have prevented it; if, indeed, there was a way in which I could have acted differently towards her long before, could have influenced the course of our lives differently – could, in effect, have been another person, could have avoided such a chaotic passage through the decade of my twenties; and I sink into maudlin reminiscence of the kind familiar to wine drinkers, wherein the past is reconfigured with the sorrowful adumbrations of excessive emotion, and before long the tears start, but I do not want to sit here like a sad bastard with my empty bottle and my memories, so I start back to the café for a refill. The same barman serves me. When I put my money on the counter, he refuses payment. It's paid for, he says, and turns to attend another customer. I spend my money on a pack of cigarettes instead, thank the barman, and return to my seat facing the cathedral.

In Pontevedra I would buy the first bottle of the day and find a convenient bench, and write through the morning, pausing for refills, until it was time to visit the free municipal restaurant in the early afternoon. Most of the writing would begin by describing a simple event or scene in my own immediate environment, and I would develop this theme with multiple variations, venturing further and deeper into the surreal or implausible, inserting spontaneous narratives with no hope of resolution, poetic descriptions glowing with an optimism that bore little relation to the profound sense of loss and loneliness I experienced most of the time.

In the amber city, wandering through streets too narrow for sunlight, the chime of church bells conveying a dense frustration, I came across a beggar without a nose, who begged a coin. I stopped to speak with him, a youngish man, with long, dirty hair. He smelled of rotting flesh. I asked what he would do with the money if I gave him some. He said he would buy wine and cigarettes. I said, in that case go, but buy two bottles, one for you, and one for me, and come back to this shady spot so we can drink together. He shuffled off, dragging one foot.

When the beggar returned, minutes later, his demeanour had changed entirely. He approached waving the bottles at me, grinning wildly. He was very low on teeth. He sat beside me in the doorway of a disused church, and as he stooped I noticed that his nearside ear was missing. Lighting a cigarette I could not fail to observe that he only had three fingers on the left hand, two on the right. It occurred to me that this was a person in the very process of disintegration.

The beggar and I drank, talking little, but I gathered he was from the south. After a while we needed to refill our bottles and walked together to the little store. On our return the tramp began to sing, deep song, a rich exuberance of sound, there in the shady alley with the watching cats and this sense of always returning to the same place: the pissed-on mattress piled against the wall, the litter of empty cartons. And this singer prince who had been consigned to the kingdom of the gutter.

I walked away, the singer in mid-song, eyes closed. He would never notice I was gone. It was not his job to notice other people's comings and goings.

34

One life is not enough for everything: but on the other hand, one life can contain too much information for a single story. A life story is akin to a weave of many stories, rather than a linear passage through time, and is complicated by the fact that few of us remain the same person throughout the course of one lifetime. This was brought home to me with particular poignancy when, over the course of several years, through what is generally termed 'recovery' (a term I am deeply suspicious of, since we are all, to some extent, in a state of recovery from something), I made the transition from vagabond poet to university researcher and lecturer, attending international conferences and staying at luxury hotels. It was not that I felt I had not earned my newfound success, or that I was not suitably qualified; I thrived in my job and worked hard at developing my knowledge and skills as an academic. In my first few years at the university, I wrote articles and papers with the energy of a neophyte, and was suitably rewarded and promoted. Nevertheless, there were still occasions when I felt like an anomaly.

In September 2000, I attended a medical conference in Barcelona and was put up at the Hotel Calderón, on the Ramblas de Catalunya. The last time I had stayed in the city, a decade earlier, home had been a park bench and my bed a flattened cardboard carton. When I took my early morning swim in the hotel's rooftop pool, I was able, after doing my lengths, to gaze down over the sprawl of Plaça de Catalunya and the Ramblas towards the Gothic quarter and the park where I had fallen ill, a decade, or a lifetime ago. At that time, momentous things had been happening in the world: the Berlin wall was coming down and the apartheid regime in South Africa was about to implode, but in a small park in Barcelona I had exhausted all my options: I had no funds left for basic survival, my self-esteem had sunk so low that I couldn't bear to cadge a bed for the night off any of the friends who were still speaking to me, and I had been evicted from the local soup kitchen for trying to stop a fight, or for starting one, I forget. Eventually, I was picked up by the city police and escorted to hospital, where I was found to be suffering from pneumonia and pleurisy.

I collapsed on arrival and was wheeled down long corridors, undergoing tests while something bleeped continuously in the background: the measure, I presumed, of my mortality. That first night I experienced a sense of detachment from my own body, an extraordinary reverse gravity, which, even in my semi-conscious state, I recognised as my arrival at some kind of final junction. I felt a desperate grief as I reflected on my wasted life. I spent three days drifting in and out of consciousness, coughing up blood, trying to get out of bed and falling over, bringing a whole apparatus of drips and intravenous leads tumbling down around me, struggling with an oxygen mask (without which I could not breathe) and having my sheets changed every few hours by efficient nurses who barely disturbed me (I was sweating so profusely that I lost several kilos in body weight). And then, one day, when I had my breath back and had regained sufficient clarity to speak coherently, there was a visit from a consultant physician, who told me that I was lucky to have survived, and that I would not be released from hospital until I was able to provide them with an address that I could go to, and evidence that I would do so. They had hidden, or disposed of my clothes, so unless I was prepared to escape across the rooftops in my regulation blue pyjamas, I had to find somewhere to go.

From the ward, I phoned my friend Lluís in Figueres, and he drove down to see me the same day. We had a long talk. Lluís told me I had issues to address. Wouldn't it be a sound idea for me to return to Wales, he suggested, where *all this started*? All this, I gathered, referred to the wreckage of my life. There were things I needed to sort out, he said, and only by returning to the source could I make a new beginning. Maybe, I agreed – inwardly aghast at the thought – but I wasn't certain there was a way back, I seemed to have lost the appetite for fresh starts. Lluís then told me I was a prisoner of duality, and that I was addicted to the notion of the epic quest. I suspected that neither one of these was a good thing.

Perversely – and with a staggering grandiosity – I had always regarded my embrace of drunkenness and aimless wandering as an intellectual or even spiritual endeavour, never merely an excuse for sloth and debauch. I saw myself as a sort of mendicant friar in the service of Dionysos. In a similar vein, I would often remark that it was not by chance that strong liquors are called 'spirits' and even at rock bottom held onto a belief that somehow the road of excess led to the palace of wisdom, to the full excoriating revelation of a burning fluid knowledge, presented by flashes of almost intolerable insight: an extraordinarily persistent and entrenched delusion that by continual inebriation I would eventually arrive at some elusive core experience – perhaps a throwback to Rimbaud and his famous insistence on a derangement of all the senses – at the same time recognising, knowing, that this was itself a trick of the drunken mind, a device by which the addicted brain could keep itself tanked up, topped up, fed with the sustaining and destructive fuel of derangement. My hangovers had long since ceased to be merely hangovers and had become instead the expression of some kind of spiritual crisis, whose resolution could only be found in more drink. I was at a dead end.

My conversation with Lluís had a profound effect on me. I didn't feel as though he was turning me away: I knew that he had touched on something important and was making his argument because he understood and cared about me. Perhaps my journey had, through its own bizarre logic, to be circular. I hadn't lived in Britain for years, and had vowed, upon last leaving, never to return. But that had been London: perhaps rural Wales would be different. Although I had only occasionally communicated with my family during the past decade, I suspected they might be willing to put me up until I was better, given the circumstances. After all, I had nearly died.

The hospital social worker contacted the British Consulate, and the following day an elderly lady resembling Miss Marple marched into my room with an armload of newspapers and magazines (the *Times* and *Telegraph*, plus supplements), an emissary from another world. I was not used to dealing with people like Miss Marple. How many times had I dragged myself, filthy and bedraggled, into consular offices in Greece or Spain, only to be turned away like a dog? Was this woman even real? As she handed me the newspapers (which I later read, absorbing the ephemera of an alien world with alternating sensations of amazement and gloom) I restrained an overwhelming desire to howl like a dog, and listened to her lay out her plans in precise tones. Miss Marple could arrange for my return to the United Kingdom, if that was what I wanted. She told me she would bring some clothes on her next visit.

I couldn't help but warm to this woman who had appeared from nowhere and whose demeanour evoked a vicarage tea party from the 1960s, and was organising my life for me. I was used to dealing with the wardens of flophouses, with officious policemen and other vindictive functionaries, with petty criminals, the dregs of street life, junkies, whores and deadbeat winos. Speaking with Miss Marple, the English language tasted foreign on my tongue.

And that was how I came to return to Wales, in 1990, and a process of reintegration and recovery began. My brother David, whom I had not seen for several years, met me at Heathrow and drove me to the family home in Crickhowell. He filled me in on Wales's chances in the forthcoming Five Nations rugby as though no time had elapsed since we had last spoken. My parents received me with kindness and I stayed with them throughout the three months of my convalescence, rediscovering, as the pains in my chest diminished, the walks around the Usk Valley and the Black Mountains that I had enjoyed as a boy. In the spring I found a place to live in Cardiff and began thinking about returning to college, to study linguistics. I met Rose one evening in June: we went back to her flat that night and have remained together ever since.

Seven years of aimless vagrancy were followed by seven years of assiduous study and rehabilitation. First I had to understand my illness, and challenge my addictive behaviours. But understanding what was wrong and actually doing anything about it were two different things. For years I had known that I was incapable of controlling my drinking, or much else in my life: I had done everything to excess for as long as I could remember. Although I was determined to break the stranglehold that addiction had on me, it was only after a long and arduous journey of false starts, relapses, attempts at control and long periods of white-knuckle sobriety that I was able to leave this dependency behind. I fought it even while accepting that I was recovering. Sometimes I lacked the resolve or the inclination to go through with it. The transition was not easy, but it became a matter of life or death. Throughout this period Rose proved a most resolute ally, refusing to be drawn into the maelstrom of co-dependency, and never allowing my illness to take control of our lives.

I cleaned up, I studied, I wrote, I became a father. Having two small children to protect and care for strengthened my resolve, took the edge off my addict's relentless egotism. I was awarded a scholarship to study for a PhD, and on the strength of it I was asked to set up a centre in health communication research at the university where I completed my doctorate. When I was thirty-nine I relapsed after a couple of years' sobriety and I signed up for rehab at a treatment centre in west Wales. I hated rehab – although not because it was tough: my experience of boarding school had been considerably tougher – and left the place after seven weeks of my twelve-week stint. But, in spite of my resistance to rehab-think and twelve-step philosophy, and although I was warned that such resistance indicated wilful pride and was a staple trick of the addictive illness (there is a strong tendency to objectify addictive illness in the AA literature), I did not agree: I knew that I was through with self-destructive drinking. Something had changed in me.

Later that year, at the age of forty, I was offered my first proper job. Now, at conferences across the globe, I spoke an exotic new language with other researchers and doctors, discussing notions such as shared decision-making in the clinical arena, and I gave lectures about the language people used in medical consultations, both doctors and patients, analysing their stories and dissecting their metaphors. I wrote about the contours and ironies of the illness experience, attempting to trace the divide between the kingdom of the sick and the kingdom of the well. I had been clean and sober for four years when I was invited to the Barcelona conference. Nevertheless, I accepted with trepidation, knowing the associations the city held for me. Those bars and cantinas of the old Barcelona had been my favourite drinking haunts anywhere on the planet. If I was going to trip up, it would be here.

I had delivered my paper at the Pompeu Fabra University, and decided to walk back to the hotel by a roundabout route, through the old part of town, rather than catch the Metro. On the way, I dropped in at the church of Santa Maria del Mar, not because I am a religious person, but because I like the building, enjoy its majestic lines, its marvellous high-vaulted ceiling, its massive pillars, its place in the mythology of the city as the 'people's church'. There were some musicians playing at the front of the church, near the altar: a cellist, a guitarist, perhaps a pianist. I sat at the edge of the south aisle and listened to the music. I had been feeling very strange since arriving in Barcelona – I was an anomaly both in the world of scholarship and the underworld of bums and winos – and this city, more than any other, delivered the sharpest possible reminder of that sense of anomaly. I did not see myself as belonging to any identifiable stratum of society, did not feel comfortable in my own skin. Back in Wales I had my family, Rose and my two young daughters, and they, more than anything, constituted my home, and gave shape to my new identity, along with my writing – I had by then published four slim collections of poetry, with limited, local success – but my family was not here now.

It was then that I saw her. She was a girl in her late teens, a gypsy waif with the aura of the streets about her, who smiled at me from where she stood near the back of the church, and then proceeded to dance down the aisle on the south side of the building, where I was leaning against a pillar, and as she passed me, bounding across the marble floor, she smiled again, a smile of such uncomplicated grace that I was left confounded. Perhaps it was the incongruity of the dancing figure in that vast and solemn temple, perhaps a welling-up of emotion at my return to a city which held many ghosts for me, the city in which a brush with death had enabled me to make my changes; but at that moment I felt as though the dancing girl had granted me a subtle gift, and that in a bizarre way Barcelona was welcoming me back.

I left the church and continued up through the Gothic quarter, wandering past my old haunts, all the relics of my old life, towards the hotel, choosing a route that crossed the Plaça de Catalunya. At this time, numerous indigents were squatting in the square in protest at the lack of facilities for homeless people, and they had spread blankets, cardboard dwellings, even the occasional tent, across a large expanse of the surface, and it was through this derelict zone that I chose to walk. I was still bathing in the glow of that angelic smile, and because I had for many years been accustomed to hanging out with derelicts and *zonards* it never crossed my mind to take a detour, to skirt the congregation of the homeless who were scattered in groups around the place. I had nothing to fear from these people. This was an oversight: I had forgotten what I had become. Dressed in a smart suit and carrying a briefcase, I presented an irresistible target. Three young men approached me, and one asked me for a cigarette. I reached in my pocket automatically, and only then did it occur to me that I might advantageously have chosen another route back to the hotel. I had barely offered the pack to the first of my interlocutors when I felt someone's hand in my coat pocket. I turned to confront the would-be thief, only to find that I was encircled, and they were moving in, crowding me out. I should have been worried, but felt strangely light-headed, as if all cause for stress had been blown away in the church of Santa Maria del Mar. Another alien hand found its way into the back pocket of my suit trousers and, brushing it away, I addressed the hand's owner with some choice phrases of gutter Spanish. The kid looked shocked, briefly, and then all three of them simply vanished, dragged away by unseen forces into the night, like phantoms sucked back into oblivion. I had just begun to feel the impending thrill of confrontation – not that I would have come well out of it, considering the odds against me – and they were gone. I looked around, expecting to see an approaching police van, or something else that would have made the youths scarper so abruptly, but there was nothing, no evidence of civic authority come to disperse my assailants. I shifted my briefcase to the other hand and walked on across the square. I was certain that the dancing girl had woven a web of invincibility around me, and that within her sanctuary no harm could come to me.

I had wanted to write a novel set in the city, and had made several false starts, but my encounter with the angel of Santa Maria del Mar gave me the impetus to continue.

Shortly after returning to Cardiff I was diagnosed with hepatitis C.

35

> Not only have I always had trouble distinguishing between
> what happened and what might have happened, but I remain
> unconvinced that the distinction, for my purposes, matters.
>
> *Joan Didion*

It is something that I never seem able to escape, this constant interweaving and interplay between the two domains of experience that constitute my life, this life which is not enough for everything. Regarding the juxtaposition of fiction and reality, or the world and literature: is it so hard to identify where one begins and the other ends? Those three would-be assailants, for example, they are no figment of the literary imagination any more than the three young Somalis outside the garage in Tudor Street were. They were real enough. These encounters are not some kind of literary conceit, a projection onto the *other* of my fear and isolation, despite the symbolic aptness of the potential assailants being three in number on both occasions. But their constituent reality only begins to make sense once the two scenes are reconstructed, refigured in writing, or in fiction, where the recurrence of the theme would be noted as a narrative ploy to nudge the reader into a realisation. Is this what literature does? Lifts an incident, or a conjunction of incidents, towards a greater truth than was ever apparent when the original lived incident or incidents occurred? If that is the case, where do we draw the line between the life story and the work of fiction?

Javier Marías begins *Dark Back of Time*, his 'false novel', with the words: "I believe I've still never mistaken fiction for reality, though I have mixed them together more than once, as everyone does, not only novelists or writers but everyone who has recounted anything since the time we know began, and no one in that known time has done anything but tell and tell, or prepare and ponder a tale, or plot one."

This eternal recounting, this need to tell and tell, is there not something appalling about it – and not only in the sense of whether or not we consciously or intentionally mix reality and fiction? Are there not times when we wish the whole cycle of telling and recounting and explaining and narrating would simply stop – if only for a week, or a day; if only for an hour? The incessant recapitulation and summary and anecdotage and repetition of things said by oneself, by others, to others, in the name of others; the chatter and the news-bearing and the imparting of knowledge and misinformation and the banter and explication and the never-ending, all-consuming barrage of blithering fatuity that pounds us from the radio, from the television, from the internet, the unceasing need to tell and make known? And whenever we recount, we inevitably embroider, invent, cast aspersion, throw doubt upon, question, examine, offer for consideration, include or discard motive, analyze, assert, make reference to, exonerate, implicate, align with, dissociate from, deconstruct, reconfigure, tell tales on, accuse, slander or lie.

There is no such thing as a literal or realistic accounting of reality. A literal understanding of reality is by definition defective, relying as it does on the perspective of literalism, the only perspective on reality that insists it is not a perspective, but a true version, *the* truth. If reality is accounted for by a literal telling, and literalism too is merely a perspective, why should we trust it? Fiction, meanwhile, does not claim to record reality, but rather, is moulded by it. According to Margaret Anne Doody, author of *The True Story of the Novel* (a nicely ironical choice of title), "one of the words for fiction [in Greek], *plasma*... is a word for images or figures in clay or wax, hence anything that is involved in imitation, a forgery; it is related to the word *plasso* ('I mould'), also the source of our word *plastic*. Fiction is a moulding and shaping, an imitation that speaks its own imitatedness, like a figurine."

Just as we do not confuse a sculpture or figurine (however exquisitely crafted) with a real-life person, when reading fiction we acknowledge that the events described did not really happen (even if they contain a wider or generic truth-value). On the other hand, we expect non-fiction or memoir to be literally true, which is why we do not easily forgive those writers who purvey tales that are pure invention and pass them off as non-fiction. But if literal truth is only ever a perspective, the truth according to that particular teller at that particular time, then we must accept that there is a blurred zone in which our understanding of reality is only an approximation, imbued with aspects of, or filaments of fictionality. This is the shadow zone, the world of the in-between, of uncertainty, ambivalence, equivocation, quandary and enchantment. We find ourselves in the hands of a memoirist or a reporter with either an underdeveloped sense of reality or an overdeveloped sense of unreality (which are not at all the same thing) – and whether or not we go along with him, or choose to trust her, will depend on a number of things, not least of which is whether or not we are enjoying the journey. In other words, our reading experience leads to an aesthetic judgement, not one based on truth-value. This, we are inclined to think, is a much more interesting place to be.

Reality and fiction can merge in and across time in at least two distinct ways. The first, more easily recognisable, is when a fictional event is founded on the actual experiences of the author. This is commonplace; indeed many authors base almost their entire oeuvre on distorted re-tellings of their own experiences. Perhaps some memorable (or insignificant) event sparks an imaginary chain of events which are devised and set down as fiction. The instigating moment is one which the author lived through; the rest is an invented concoction following on from that moment or event. And at other times – and these are the ones which I wish to address – a fictional event or perception or concept is reproduced in reality *after* the story, or poem, or literary artifice, has been put down on paper. In grammar, cataphora is the reference to a textual item that has not yet been mentioned. By extension we might consider cataphoric reference also to be the way phenomena sometimes manifest themselves in the world after they have been written. On these occasions it is as if the workings of the inner world, the confabulations of the writer, had somehow seeped through into the outer world; as if there were a reflective symmetry between the devices of the imagination and events in reality, a kind of sympathetic magic, which is the idea that you can influence an outcome by concentrating your energy on an analogous object, invoking the desired effect through similitude. Georges Bataille refers to something of the kind when he describes writing as a form of contagion, the conjuring of contagious energies. This can happen either by accident or intentionally. Our ancestors practised a variety of sympathetic magic by painting buffalo on the walls of their caves, acting out the hunt before it began, in the effort to secure a favourable outcome. But it can also happen without any such intentionality on the part of the protagonist, or author.

Sometimes – in other words – there is a traffic between the world of reality and the less well-regulated zones of the imagination, and it is hard to find explanations that do not take refuge in the bland holdall of coincidence. For instance, a few weeks ago I believe I conjured Hubert Tsarko simply by writing about him. I had not heard from him in eighteen months but the day after writing about him in this account, he phoned me. This seems to happen far too often to ascribe it to mere chance: you think of someone, and they call on the telephone. But perhaps we only remember these occasions because of the thousands of times we think of someone and they do *not* call. So let's consider another line of inquiry.

A friend of mine once began writing a story about a young woman who moves into a new flat in which an ancient desk has been left behind by previous occupants, a desk inscribed by graffiti and obscene carvings. When she was a third of the way into the work, which she now imagined as a novella, she moved apartment, and to her dismay (and secret delight) the only article of furniture in the front room of the flat was a huge scarred desk. Her real-life landlord, too, behaved like the landlord in her story, and even looked like him. My friend was so impressed by the turn of events that she titled the novella 'Desk'.

Something not dissimilar has occurred to me. A couple of years ago I was writing a story about alchemy, one which required me to do a good deal of reading about the subject, and I became particularly interested in the life of a seventeenth-century Welsh alchemist called Thomas Vaughan, who grew up near Crickhowell. Vaughan is supposed to have died while cooking mercury in one of his alchemical experiments. I read up on the uses of mercury in alchemy and its relationship in mythology to the eponymous god, Mercurius, known to the Greeks as Hermes, the god of communication, as well as of commerce and of flight. One afternoon, while deep in my studies, I went down to the kitchen of my house to prepare some food, and there on the table I spotted some small silver globules, which rolled under my fingers when touched. It was mercury. I thought for a moment that I was going crazy. The house was empty. There was nothing else on the table to explain the presence of the mercury. It was only later, when my daughter returned home, that I discovered what had happened. She had taken a thermometer out of its case, dropped it, and it had broken. She cleaned up the glass, but had not spotted the mercury that had spilled out and rolled across the table. So, a rational explanation was provided – but it did not explain the fortuitous, temporal nature of the event: why that particular accident on that particular day?

In 1995 I had completed a short collection of poetry, which was translated into Catalan by Montserrat Lunati and illustrated by my friend Lluís Peñaranda. The idea was to make a nicely-crafted bilingual art product. To this end we decided to publish the collection ourselves, under our own imprint. After obtaining some modest funding, we decided on the name *Cranc* as appropriate for our publishing house (the word means 'crab' in both Welsh and Catalan) and in June of that year I set off to Spain to attend the launch – there was to be an exhibition of Lluís' illustrations in the village of Cistella – and to pick up the books, as they were being printed in nearby Girona. As I left my house in Cardiff to get into the taxi for the airport, a crab landed at my feet with a smack, dropped from a great height by a passing gull. Although there are many seagulls in Cardiff, and my house is near the bay, in eighteen years no crab has ever been deposited anywhere near my person from aloft *except on the day that I was setting off to pick up 250 poetry books published under the imprint of the crab.*

There is no point in trying to establish some causal relationship between the purpose of that trip (beginning with my journey from front door to taxi) and the appearance of the airborne crab, any more than one can rationally account for the appearance of a large battered desk in my friend's new apartment, or the timeliness of my daughter's accident with the mercury. Jung coined the term 'synchronicity' to account for examples of *meaningful* coincidence such as these, and to differentiate them, I suppose, from 'commonplace' coincidences, that is, random events that carry no meaningful impact or resonance.

To say that we mix reality and fiction is one thing, but to accept that reality and the workings of the imagination are in permanent dialogue with each other – that is something quite different. I can accept that while reality and the workings of the imagination form distinct realms of experience, they also form a dualistic construct that underpins our experiencing of the world. I cannot claim to understand how this happens, but I know that it does: I know that it happens all the time.

36

Reality favours symmetries and slight anachronisms.

Jorge Luís Borges

In May 2005, immediately after the launch party for my Barcelona novel, in which the protagonist is abducted into a sinister cult, I flew to a publishers' conference in Buenos Aires, and was promptly immersed in a real case of abduction, involving a member of my family.

I had been invited by Gabriela Adorno, who runs the literature section of an international arts foundation. The week was to be packed with meetings with publishers, editors, agents and literary journalists. I was asked to attend by the publishers for whom I was poetry editor at the time. Although I was no expert in modern Latin American literature, I was passionate about Borges, and knew enough to recognise that Argentine literature in the last fifty years has been dominated by what one critic has called "Borges' terrible shadow". I was also a fan of his compatriot Julio Cortazar, the second major figure in modern Argentine fiction, who escaped that terrible shadow by living and working in Paris, and I had read a fair range of other Latin American authors.

I woke from a temazepam sleep over southern Brazil and looked down on the dark moss of the receding forest far below in the tangerine light of sunrise, then at the green-grey pampas and the huge serpentine channel of the Rio Plata down towards the sea. Buenos Aires sprawled below us as the plane banked and I took off my headphones and closed my eyes. At the airport my niece, Nicky, was there to meet me as I came through customs, looking tired, up all night but sweet and fine and happy. She was twenty-five, had found a new direction in Buenos Aires, and it was important to her, as if she'd also found some kind of resolution to her restlessness as a developing writer. In my hotel room I unpacked, showered and lay down on the crisp white sheets of my double bed. The television's 64 channels proved too much of a challenge, so I opted for the familiar and watched the FA Cup final from the Millennium Stadium, a game whose outcome meant nothing to me. I flicked through a city guide. Later, I ate lunch in the hotel restaurant. Alongside the fantastically tender, buttery steak were Andes potatoes, which elicit a peculiar sense of longing for a taste almost but not entirely forgotten: small, floury, sweet, mineral-rich: the texture of the earth from which they are grown.

Of all Borges' stories, the author's own favourite was 'The South'. He once commented that this story could be read in two ways: in one, all the events are presumed to have occurred as they are described in the text; in another, the second half of the story is the hallucination of the protagonist. The first half, which we can take as a literal reading, tells of a man named Dahlmann who suffers an accident and is taken to hospital with a serious case of septicemia. In the second half, he leaves hospital and takes a train to his family's disused ranch in the south, the mythical south of the title. On arrival at a small railway station near his destination, he encounters a group of local toughs, with one of whom he fights, and he is killed.

When our lives are most likely to follow preordained patterns, following a timetable laid out for us by others, it often appears that there is another, darker agenda at work, which does everything in its power to shift and sway, to unbalance the course of events that we had expected to take place. This result is what might best be compared to a series of hallucinations, or, as in the Borges story, a forking of paths, a multiplicity of outcomes. We are led to question whether Dahlmann 'in fact' dies under the surgeon's knife (in which case the rest of the story is a prolonged hallucination experienced during his last moments) or is the development that Borges describes only one of a series of possible outcomes, a tracking of the protagonist through just one of innumerable universes? My first night in Buenos Aires brought home to me the fact that such questions are not purely theoretical, but have the immediacy and force of terrifying reality.

After taking a stroll around the barrio I returned to my hotel and sent some emails to family and friends in Wales. At 8.30pm Nicky arrived at the hotel and we walked towards the famous cemetery of Recoleta, where Borges' family is buried. There was a chill in the air, and after leaving Europe in springtime it was strange to see the signs of autumn, pavements dotted with fallen golden leaves. We found a place to eat. Nicky told me she had recently been offered work as the Buenos Aires *Time Out* tango correspondent. Dance was, for her, a lifelong love. We had plenty to catch up on. It was good just to eat and chat, talk family, talk books: I wasn't sure how much free time there would be in the week ahead; the timetable for the publishing conference was packed.

As the evening wore on, Nicky seemed a little concerned about the time. I suspected she had a date and I didn't want to be a killjoy. Around midnight we left the restaurant and deliberated on whether or not to share a taxi, dropping me off at my hotel on her way back to San Telmo, where she lived in a hostel. There was a row of taxis across the road and Nicky got in the back of one. I hesitated before deciding instead to walk back to the hotel: it would help me orient myself.

In Borges' story I find these words at the start of the second paragraph: *Blind to a fault, destiny can be ruthless at one's slightest distraction.* Why did I not know that I should have got into the taxi with her? Was my intuition taking a break, or, as in the conceit of the soul travelling at the pace of a trotting camel, had my own soul simply not caught up with me, delayed, as it were, by the speed of my Boeing's flight across the south Atlantic? Would it have made any difference if we had taken the taxi together as far as my hotel? She would, after all, still have driven off with the taxi driver, but he would, perhaps, have been wary: I would have a full description of him and might well have taken the number of the cab (probably an irrelevance as it turned out). Worse still, the fact later haunted me that she would not have got into that particular taxi on that particular night had I not arrived in Buenos Aires on that particular day. But at this point, the innumerable patterns of possibility and probability begin to kick in and you realise that this way madness lies. You can, if you are so disposed, trace such concatenations back to the moment of conception and beyond, to those of one's parents and distant ancestors, to the first amoebas. There is no point in going there.

I thought maybe I'd stop off for a drink in one of the many bars that lined the streets along the way, but in the end decided to walk straight back to the hotel. It had been a long day, a long week in fact, and I wanted to sleep. My sense of direction, like my intuition, was not as brilliant as I had thought it was. I managed to find the street where my hotel was located, but started walking towards the wrong end and ended up going a mile or so out of my way. I finally arrived back an hour and a quarter later.

As I came into the hotel room, the telephone was ringing. I picked up and a doctor introduced herself. She spoke in faltering English. She asked me if I was Nicky's uncle and told me that my niece had been involved in an incident. I asked her to continue in Spanish and got directions to the hospital. It was a public facility on the other side of town, called Hospital Argelich. She told me that my niece was injured but conscious, and was asking for me. I hurried downstairs and ordered a taxi from the hotel reception. Half an hour later I was at the hospital, a grim, labyrinthine building, and eventually tracked Nicky down in a treatment room. A nurse was cleaning her face, which was caked with blood. I was told that probably both her ankles were broken, that they were awaiting the x-ray results. Otherwise, Nicky appeared to be intact, though it was difficult to ascertain for sure, since shock can produce highly variable responses in different people. She told me her story.

Almost immediately after setting off, the taxi driver had begun to drive in a direction that did not lead to San Telmo. Nicky, who knew the city well enough after three months, began to complain. The driver was taciturn. Nicky became suspicious, then frightened. As the car began to leave the city, she realised something was seriously wrong. The driver was speaking in a low voice into a mobile phone, and the cab radio was not switched on. She guessed later he must have been arranging a rendezvous with an accomplice. But for now, she resumed her argument with the driver, more volubly, who told her to be quiet, then, from the glove compartment, produced a pistol, which he waved in her direction, uttering threats. The car had reached the multi-lane highway leading out of the city, and Nicky was very scared. Leaning forward, she screamed at the driver, who grabbed her hair, attempting to force her head down, out of view of passing vehicles, while still clutching the pistol and trying to steer the car with the other hand. With the realisation that she was now the victim of an abduction, and the horrifying possibilities that came with it, came the certainty that she must escape, whatever that might involve. Her actions from this point took on an aspect of single-minded determination: to get out of that car and away from her captor in whatever way she could. The doors of the car were centrally locked, so while struggling with the driver, she worked down the rear window. The driver shouted at her, but despite pulling her hair, was unable to control her movements, and the car swerved across the road, coming close to colliding with a van. Taking advantage of his efforts to retain control of the vehicle, she pulled free and hurled herself headfirst through the rear window. The car was travelling at speed. She must have twisted in mid-air to avoid landing on her head, because although sustaining head wounds, it was her feet that took the major impact on landing. She did not lose consciousness, but started running (on broken ankles, as it turned out) back towards the city, terrified that the taxi driver would recapture her, or shoot her, in an attempt to force her back into his car. There was not much traffic on the highway, and besides, she must have presented a scary spectacle, face streaming blood, as she tried to flag down vehicles. Someone stopped, maybe the third or fourth car to pass. She collapsed on the hard shoulder and the driver wrapped his coat over her shoulders and called an ambulance on his cell phone. Thus it was that she arrived, stretchered, in a neck-brace, at the Hospital Argelich.

At certain points of crisis, everyday perceptions tend to be suspended in a state of exacerbated intensity. Borges again: *In the obscurity, something brushed by his forehead: a bat, a bird? On the face of the woman who opened the door to him he saw horror engraved, and the hand he wiped across his face came away red with blood. The edge of a recently painted door which someone had forgotten to close had caused this wound. Dahlmann was able to fall asleep, but from the moment he awoke at dawn the savour of all things was atrociously poignant.* So it was in the Hospital Argelich. Every instant was pregnant with imminent, but frustrated lucidity.

I knew about Argentina's economic crisis, knew that public funding for health care was not comparable to European levels, but this place was like a nightmarish parody of a hospital A & E department. I leaned against a table in the treatment room only to notice that its surface was caked with dried blood. The floors and walls needed washing. A young medic passed by, and briefly discussed the finer points of an x-ray which he clearly did not understand. Someone applied plaster of Paris to Nicky's legs, from the knees down. It was like watching a child slapping wet clay into some shapeless monstrosity. I wondered if any of the staff had received anything other than the most basic training. They carried out their duties with the scantest regard to basic hygiene, only occasionally donning sterile gloves. The doctor who had phoned me could not be found. She had moved on to another emergency, or else had gone home. It dawned on me that this was a hospital without doctors. I felt the heavy burden of privilege, of coming from a rich country in which certain essentials are taken for granted and with that sense of privilege came a peculiar sort of guilt. Who, after all, were we to demand anything of this country's services, crippled as it was by debts brought on, at least in some degree, by the inequalities of the global economy directed by the world's richest countries, from one of which I held a passport?

A cheerful young man stitched up the bloody mess at the back of Nicky's head, then applied himself to the bridge of the nose, where a couple more sutures were required. Bizarrely, I have a photo of this on my phone. He was talkative and good at his job. Then, without explanation, Nicky was taken from room to room in an ancient wheelchair pushed by a lame midget in his seventies, and I trundled behind. At each corner and doorway the midget banged into an adjacent wall or doorjamb, knocking Nicky's ankle. When I tried to push the chair myself, the lame one told me that this was his duty, and there was something so tragic about his earnestness and sense of dedication amid all the hospital's random carnage that I let it pass, positioning myself between the ankle and any obstacles that the wheelchair expert might have to negotiate. As we passed down corridors, screams could be heard from behind shut doors. Everything seemed suspended in a state of reluctant animation. I spoke at length with a police sergeant called Segovia, who referred to me by the honorific *Caballero*, painstakingly filled out forms, and told me that in two days' time I must report to Police Commissariat 16, which covered the zone of the city where the 'incident' had taken place, in order to procure a full report and denunciation. I was handed a prescription for Nicky by one of the medics, and instructed in how to administer anti-tetanus injections. The prescription also detailed some analgesics and antibiotics that I was to give her. Then we left. Out into the autumnal morning.

> The first tang of autumn, after the summer's oppressiveness, seemed like a symbol in nature of [Dahlmann's] rescue and release from fever and death. The city, at seven in the morning, had not lost that air of an old house lent it by the night; the streets seemed like long vestibules, the plazas were like patios... a second before his eyes registered the phenomena themselves, he recalled the corners, the billboards, the modest variety of Buenos Aires. In the yellow light of the new day, all things returned to him.

I took Nicky back to her hostel and then returned to my own hotel and tried, unsuccessfully, to sleep. I had a meeting with the conference organisers and explained what had happened the night before. They insisted that my first duty was to my niece, and if I was unable to attend the conference, they would collect the necessary materials from publishers and literary agents for me to study at a later time. I was due to speak at a press conference later in the week about the state of publishing and translation in Wales but, again, was told that I should only attend if it was remotely possible. I was in a highly emotional state by now and felt inordinately grateful to Gabriela, who had spent months organising and trying to fund this conference, grateful for her understanding and her offers of help.

That night I took several sleeping pills and was drifting into slumber when the phone rang again. It was a friend of Nicky's from the hostel, a Portuguese photographer called Tiago Venancio, telling me that Nicky was in a lot of pain. Another rush to the Hospital Argelich, this time with the help of Tiago, and it took the two of us to carry Nicky up and down stairs with no wheelchair access. The A & E department was crawling with human wreckage, specimens of lost humanity, many of them calling out in agony – a scene from Dante's *Inferno*, commented Tiago. Somehow we managed to ascertain the whereabouts of an orthopaedic specialist, asleep on the fifth floor. Tiago hammered on the door of the ward he was attached to, and a young doctor appeared. He cut open the plaster of Paris on the leg that was causing most of

167

the pain. The plaster on her right leg had been put on incorrectly, he told us, crushing against the ankle bone rather than supporting it. I had the x-rays from the night before. He examined them and said that both feet needed operating on immediately. However, he continued, it would not be possible to do this here: they had neither the staff nor the beds. So what should I do? I asked. Get her into a private hospital, he answered. There were several that specialised in orthopaedic work of this kind.

In the course of the day, again with the help of Gabriela, I managed to locate a private hospital. By the time we arrived thirty-six hours had elapsed since Nicky's injury and she was in dire pain. In contrast to the Argelich, the German Hospital was a caricature of Teutonic efficiency. This was where the rich people came, and those of us from countries with currencies that could profit from the lamentable state of the Argentinian peso. Within five minutes of arrival we were in a consulting room with three orthopaedic surgeons. I felt like weeping with relief. Over the next week Nicky underwent a complicated but successful operation and began to make a steady recovery. Of course, this was not always a smooth process; Nicky needed to recover from more than the physical injuries. But within six months she was dancing again.

This narrative of my niece's abduction can, like Borges' story, be read in two ways: in one, all the events are presumed to have occurred as they are described in the text; in another, the second half of the unwritten story is the hallucination of the protagonist. The first half, which we can take as a literal reading, tells of a young woman who is abducted by an armed desperado who has stolen a taxi: she escapes from the speeding car, ends up in hospital, has an operation, and returns to recuperate with her family in Wales. Even her fear that she would not dance again proves to be groundless. In the second, mercifully unscripted version, she is taken to an unknown destination and disappears from human history, from human life (although, in an interminable agony of irresolution that mirrors that of Argentina's own *desaparecidos*, not from the memories of those who loved her). But the scope of the human tragedy implicit in this story is not limited to me, to my niece, or to our relatively comfortable and well-nourished lives. The epidemic of *secuestros*, of abductions, kidnappings, rape, enforced prostitution and murder is increasing, not only across Latin America but in many countries across the world.

My trip to Buenos Aires turned into a sleepless week of taxi rides between hospitals, police stations and government institutions, trying to secure the paperwork necessary to pursue a 'denunciation' of the crime. On my last evening there, after being misdirected to three consecutive commissariats I finally got the piece of paper I needed (with no help from the British Consulate, whose officials had decided to take a four-day holiday). But I was able to spend one evening, my last, at a *milonga* with my fellow editors, in Palermo Viejo, the barrio where Borges grew up. Walking from a workers' canteen, talking with the Turkish publisher Halil Beyta about the great poet Nazim Hikmet, I felt saddened that I had missed out on the week's conference in this passionate, fantastic city. But by the grilled window of the club's entrance, with an almost gratuitous sense of occasion, sat a black cat. She arched her back for me to stroke her. I was aware, not for the first time, of the strange truth that events in life sometimes begin as fiction and are replicated only later in fact. Borges again: *[He] thought, as he smoothed the cat's black coat, that this contact was an illusion and that the two beings, man and cat, were as good as separated by a glass, for man lives in time, in succession, while the magical animal lives in the present, in the eternity of the instant.*

37

Roberto Bolaño wrote a strange, poignant article shortly before he died, part-essay, part-monologue, originally intended for delivery at a conference in Spain, and dedicated to the writer's hepatologist. There are two things that strike me as remarkable about the piece, and the first concerns its title. It is called 'Literature + Illness = Illness', a provocative equation which suggests that illness is a constant; whatever it is conjoined with, whatever culture lobs at it, however its victims choose to define it, illness remains itself, and resists appropriation.

The second concerns the notion of the journey, or of travel, which was a defining feature of Bolaño's own life, as was illness. In the essay, the journey *is* illness, a path which many of us must travel. This is, of course, a paradox, since the journey is also the prime metaphor for life itself.

I believe the essay serves as Roberto's final testament and homage to poetry, which he always considered his true medium. It seems significant that the article ever got written at all, since Bolaño was at the time – as he had been for several years – immersed in the final drafts of his masterpiece, *2666*, and living, as his friend Andrés Neuman wrote, "like a dying man making his farewells". And he wrote, according to Neuman, "with the fury of last chances, with the vital melancholy of the gravely ill".

Bolaño begins by explaining his absence from the conference at which he is supposed to be delivering his speech, on the grounds that he is too ill to attend. He then goes on a roundabout account of a recent visit to his hepatologist where he receives bad news – very bad news – about his illness, and how, on stepping back into the waiting room after his consultation, he momentarily sees, or hallucinates, all the patients there to be crawling around the floor on all fours, like beasts. In fact, he becomes so absorbed in this visual aberration or fantasy that he barely takes in the presence of another doctor, who asks him to come along with her and take some tests. Still reeling from his interview with the hepatologist, Bolaño gives the impression that he would rather not be subjected to any further tests, but in a state of shock at seeing the waiting-room slithering with quadrupedal human life, he agrees – "I have no idea why, but in the end I said yes."

I ponder over the text as I read this, since I cannot tell whether Bolaño is temporarily deranged after the diagnosis, as he claims, and is describing a spontaneous hallucination, or whether he is using the allegory of sick patients dragging themselves across the waiting-room floor to evoke a Beckettian landscape in which humanity is condemned to crawl about in the primeval slime like lizards. The image is a shocking one, but perhaps not so strange to me, bringing to mind as it does the A & E Department of the Hospital Argelich in Buenos Aires.

Bolaño is then led by the diminutive doctor (he emphasises her size, remarking on it three times) into an enormous lift, "the biggest lift that I have seen in my life, a lift into which a shepherd could have led a small flock of sheep and a herdsman two mad cows and a nurse two empty trolley beds". This vast lift, along with endless corridors, queues of patients, and crowded waiting rooms, is another emblem of the de-humanizing architecture of the modern hospital. We step into a huge iron crate that manoeuvres between floors, each of which is designated to host a different category of sick people or to research and treat infirmities with terrible names. A hospital visit for the chronically ill patient also typically involves being shuffled from department to department for a variety of tests. In the assessment week that I spent at Birmingham's Queen Elizabeth Hospital in February I was tested for lung damage, heart damage, kidney damage and brain damage, for which purpose I was transported down many corridors and in several lifts (or the same lift many times, it makes no difference, since during those somnolent journeys one does not really recognise the scenery, even if one has made the journey a dozen times before). Like Roberto, I had to undertake the test of the upright fingers – a procedure devised for patients with liver failure – which consisted of extending my hands out in front of me vertically for a few seconds, fingers pointing upwards, the backs facing me. The point of the exercise is that at a more advanced phase of the disease it is impossible to maintain the fingers in this posture: they simply fold in. "The day that my fingers cannot remain upright," wrote

Bolaño, "I don't know quite what I will do, although I know for sure that I will not do it." But these tests must be done, and part of the ritual of testing involves traversing numerous horizontal and vertical corridors within the hospital building.

Inside the lift is an empty trolley bed, and Bolaño, "whether in sound judgement or in a moment of rashness", realises that he is attracted to the tiny doctor, and he wonders – in a tone hovering between detachment and dismay – what would happen if he suggested to her that they make love there and then in the lift, "seeing as there was no shortage of beds". This (unvoiced) thought sets off another, and Bolaño recalls a scene from a film (*Dead Man Walking*) in which Susan Sarandon, disguised as a nun, reproachfully asks Sean Penn how he could be thinking about sex when he only has a few days to live. Bolaño considers her question to be preposterous since, to his mind, sex "is the one thing that those condemned to die *are* going to want", a theory that he expands upon in some detail: "A good screw is the one thing that the occupants of prisons and hospitals crave. The impotent simply and solely want to screw. The castrated simply and solely want to screw. The gravely wounded, the suicides, the unrepentant followers of Heidegger. Even Wittgenstein, who is the greatest philosopher of the twentieth century, the only thing he wanted was to screw. Even the dead, I read somewhere, only want to screw. It's sad to have to admit to it, but that's the way it is." At which stage, the reader might justifiably wonder where on earth Bolaño is heading with this: but where he leads us is to the primal motivations behind poetry, sex being the second rung on the ladder of a poetic apprenticeship (the first being travel, and the third, books).

But most particularly – in a seismic shift that should come as no surprise to his readers by now – Bolaño wants us to consider the ideas underlying the great French poetry of the latter part of the nineteenth century, which he judges to be the high-water mark of European poetic expression. Exploring poems by Mallarmé and Baudelaire, Bolaño is convinced that sex, travel and books form an intimate experiential triad that these French poets exploited to the full, and which Bolaño himself comes to recognise as the formal equation that drives his own work. And even though travel, sex and books are roads that lead nowhere, we have to lose ourselves in them in order to return with *something*, whatever that may be.

He asks us to consider the opening lines of Baudelaire's great poem, Le Voyage, which he sees as epitomising this poetic expression:

One day we leave, with fire in the brain,
Heart great with rancour, bitter in its mood;
Outward we travel on the rolling main,
Lulling infinity in finitude:

Some gladly flee their homelands gripped in vice;
Some, horrors of their childhood, others still –
Astrologers lost in a woman's eyes –
Some perfumed Circe with a tyrant's will.

Not to become a beast, each desperate one
Makes himself drunk on space and blazing skies;
The gnawing ice, the copper-burning sun
Efface the scars of kisses and of lies.

But the true voyagers set out to sea
Just for the leaving's sake; hearts lift aloft,
Nothing dissuades them from their destiny,
Something beyond their knowing cries, "We're off!"

"In a way," writes Bolaño, "the journey that the crew of Baudelaire's poem are embarked on resembles the voyage of the damned. I am going to travel, I am going to lose myself in unknown territories, to see what I will find, to see what happens. But first, I am going to renounce everything. Or what amounts to the same thing: in order to truly travel the travellers must have nothing to lose. The journey... resembles the journey the sick person makes aboard his trolley bed, from his room to the operating theatre, where beings with their faces hidden behind masks await him, like bandits from the sect of the *Hashishin*."

Writing, which became for Bolaño not only the focus of his resistance to illness but the expression of his longing for survival, provides a kind of salvation. I put down Bolaño's text with a new understanding of his words: "returning to the beginning, knowing full well that the journey and the travellers are condemned."

The trope of the journey finds its ultimate expression in illness. Illness is itself the journey. The equation by which the article is titled, *Literature + Illness = Illness*, might therefore be applied to both the other passions of the writer: *Sex + Illness = Illness*; *Travel + Illness = Illness*. Illness as *n*, where *n* is the constant in any equation. It pains me to accept it, but it is true. It is the way in which the driving forces of sex and travel and, of course, literature culminate in the experience of illness that appals and fascinates me: it is not simply that this is what happens to us, but that this is what we ourselves become, those of us who loved maps as children, and who one day set out on blind and aimless journeys, only to wind up bereft — but with luck, not self-pitying — the remnants of one's identity tied together in a makeshift splint, being pushed down a corridor on a trolley bed.

Outside my attic room, I seem to hear threads of accordion music and echoing laughter drift past on the night air.

38

graft *noun* A piece of living tissue surgically transplanted to another place on the same organism, or to another organism, so that it might adhere and grow; the process of transplanting tissue for this purpose.

OED

On 26th April 2007, I receive the call. It is half past nine in the evening, a Thursday. I am about to settle down with my wife and daughters to watch a DVD of David Lynch's *Elephant Man*, an inspired choice under the circumstances, given how oedema and ascites have transformed and bloated my body.

The transplant coordinator, calling from the liver unit in Birmingham, tells me that I should get ready to come in at once; the liver that has been donated is, the surgeons think, ideal for me. The donor had suffered from and been treated for the viral hepatitis that I too carry, but this is not a problem, since a hepatitis-infected liver can safely be transplanted to a patient who is hepatitis C positive (HCV+), as the new liver will, in any case, become infected. Our tissue types and blood groups match up. The operation, the *graft*, will take place first thing in the morning. I say I will be along as soon as I am able.

I did not expect the call so soon. Somewhere along the line, after discussions with staff at the liver unit, I have mentally booked myself in for around August. Of course, I was told there was no way of knowing when the call would come, as it depends on so many factors – but I certainly did not expect it that mild April evening as I prepared to settle down with John Hurt's heartrending portrayal of John Merrick. On putting down the receiver I say to Rose, "They've got a liver for me." The words sound not only ridiculous, but strained, over-familiar, as though I were following a rather fanciful script; my voice is cracked and I think as I speak: *I sound like someone else.*

I try to conjure a mental picture of the donor. The coordinator has given me the minimum of detail. I know that, at forty-two, he was younger than me, that he had been treated for hepatitis C, and that he had suffered a brain haemorrhage, but nothing else. I feel a surge of compassion for this stranger, and for his bereaved family, and of gratitude to them all, but the sentiment is temporarily swamped by the momentousness of the task ahead of us. Rose and I make rushed phone calls. The literature from the liver unit advises that one keep an overnight bag packed and ready: of course I haven't, so I scramble essential toiletries into a holdall, and throw in pyjamas, slippers, a couple of books, an ipod.

We have to make a detour on our way to Birmingham, to drop off the girls and the dog with my sister, who lives in the Monmouthshire countryside. We arrange to meet at our dad's house in Crickhowell, where we grew up. When we arrive, just over an hour later, my sister pats my swollen belly, and says that it's a bit like going in to have a baby. I am unsure quite how I feel about this analogy.

Once we have said our farewells and hugged the girls several times over, Rose and I continue our journey. It is past midnight by the time we leave Crickhowell. We are behind schedule because of the detour. The roads to Birmingham are practically empty. There is something almost sacred in the character of the journey: I think of the sanctity of the gladiator on the eve of battle. It seems somehow *right* to be speeding down these empty roads in the dead of night. For a part of the way, near the start of the drive, a forest crowds up to the edge of the road: since early childhood this has been a fabulous zone for me, an archetypal woodland which I once imagined to be inhabited by goblins and wolves and armless maidens. As we motor up the wooded hill, it seems to me as if these hidden, luminescent beings are emerging from the shadows to urge me onward, fuelling me with guile and valour. It seems fitting, too, that the big old Peugeot willingly exceeds the speed limit almost the whole way, on a road littered with speed traps, but we are not once flashed. This all augurs well. We arrive at the hospital at a quarter to two in the morning, having made the trip in record time. The temperature has dropped: it is several degrees colder here than in Cardiff.

I am admitted to the liver ward and told that I will be undergoing various last-minute tests, specifically to check whether any of the excess fluid that has collected on my belly is infected in any way.

This takes an age, and in the end the two doctors give up as they are unable to draw off an adequate sample for testing. However, being on the lookout for omens of any kind, I am reassured to know that this paucity of liquid residue is probably a good sign.

I know the staff on this ward, having spent a week here in February for the physical assessment test to ascertain whether I was a suitable candidate for transplant. Being on friendly terms with the nurses from my recent visit makes the experience familiar and unthreatening. I turn to Rose, who is seated in an armchair at my bedside and tell her I am going to try and get some sleep. She wraps herself in my coat and does the same.

Around the time of change of shift on the ward, at seven, we are visited by the anaesthetist, who introduces himself and gives a short account of his duties, followed by the surgeon himself, Professor W. He exudes calmness and benign authority. Rose and I agree that he is a person whose competence is unquestionable and in whose hands I will be safe. He is wearing a nice suit.

Being manoeuvred down hospital corridors on a trolley bed has little to recommend it: you are now indisputably cast in the role of *subject* – you have become the one to whom *things are done*. This sense of utter helplessness is a challenge both to dignity and identity: you are simply the poor sod on the trolley whom passers-by will avoid looking at too closely. In the lift the other passengers stare at the ceiling, and I think of Hannibal Lecter. And then, the thought occurs to me that I spent ten years studying and writing about the subjectivity of the patient, that I have a PhD in the narrative construction of illness experience, have published in learned journals and even written a couple of books on the subject. None of this can help me now. I am in a post-discursive zone. I have reached the End of Theory.

Once inside the operating rooms, the situation becomes increasingly non-negotiable: the anaesthetist greets me by name but I have difficulty recognising him, transformed as he is by mask and surgical overalls. The surgeon too pops up with a consoling reminder: "I realise this is a big thing for you, but just remember that for us here, this is what we do every day." He smiles. I do not panic. I am calm. I reason that if something does go wrong, I probably won't know about it. Then the anaesthetist approaches once more, gives me an injection, and as he pulls away, the world goes with him.

I thought I had woken from a dream of the sea, but the waking was a part of the dream and instead I found myself upon a makeshift raft, the ocean swelling placidly around me, sharing tuna sandwiches with my dog. We rock unsteadily on the raft. I scour the horizon for any hint of land. Night is falling. I can hear nothing, and the gravity of silence makes me turn: a massive liner is bearing down, a million lights ablaze along the bows, lights that flicker into knowledge of something vast, unstoppable.

Coming to in intensive care, I nudge close to the surface several times before breaking through the last waves of sleep and opening my eyes. It is the afternoon of the next day. I am parched and my throat hurts, but I am evidently alive. I ask for water from the patient and fastidious Filipino male nurse who hovers at my bedside. My intake is restricted to occasional sips, which I swill around my mouth before swallowing for maximum lubrication, but I am impatient to drink, and inevitably take in more water than I am permitted. My nurse chides me gently, tells me again to take small sips.

I have often wondered, prior to the operation, how it would feel to be in a hospital bed immediately post-op, knowing that another person's liver lies inside my body. At this same hospital, in February, I met successful, long-term transplant patients, and in spite of their apparent normality and good health, in spite of what I had been told about the advances made in transplant surgery, I could not help but regard these survivors as freakish cyborgs: insubstantial beings held together by pins and tape – and now I was one of them. Awkwardly, I pull back the bedclothes to look at my torso. Below the gauze bandage I follow the contours of a ridge that snakes across my stomach where the metal clips are planted (later, when the bandage is removed, I count fifty-one). Even more than during recent weeks, I feel at a remove from my own physical person, this immovable object to which I am attached and which now contains a large element of the not-me. The singularity of this sensation is perhaps due to the fact that nothing in my experience has been remotely similar: I have nothing to gauge it by. This lump inside my body is almost palpable otherness, and yet, if I did not know that I had received another man's liver, would I feel any different? Would I *know*? Because of the drugs I am being fed, the only area of real discomfort in my body centres on my sore throat and the intolerable dryness of my mouth. Otherwise, it is too early for me to register any emotion other than relief that I have come through and am being told the operation has been a grand success.

I endure my thirst with a martial, dogged humour. Rose sits by my side, a warm and subtle presence, and I enjoy the visit of the surgeon, Professor W, and ask him when the monstrous battery of farts that issues forth from me might ease up. He tells me – and this is a little alarming – that the new liver was uncommonly large, coming in at 1.2 kilogrammes (the average liver weighs 0.7 kg). He says that with time it will shrink to accommodate to my body size, just as, if I had received a smaller organ – or half an organ, which is commonly the case – it would grow to fill the designated space. I have a sudden desire to mourn my old liver. It served me well, I think, sentimentally, before it finally gave up the ghost. Professor W says he had a hell of a job getting it out, which, quite apart from serving as a metaphor for the extinction of a past life, evokes some horrible imagery. I like the Prof – he has a nice sense of the macabre which he can't quite keep in check, like his smile when discussing my prolific flatulence, marking him out as someone I might get along with well in civilian life.

At night, my temperature rises suddenly and I feel the onset of fear for the first time since entering the hospital: a dense fear, cloudy and dull, loitering, it seems, just to the back and to the left of me, like the devil. I am feverish. I fear I might have contracted some iatrogenic infection such as MRSA; I fear my body might be rejecting the new liver. I do not manage to sleep much that night, in spite of the medication, anxious in case my temperature continues to rise, putting me at threat of I know not what. There is a remote possibility of having to undergo more surgery if things go wrong, even a chance that I might require another new liver, for which an emergency, Europe-wide call would have to be sent out; but when my temperature is taken the next morning, it has fallen. I am off the critical list. That evening I am transferred to the special care unit, a halfway house between intensive

179

care and the general ward. The following afternoon I manage to get out of bed and into an armchair. My father and sister visit, and they bring my daughters, Sioned and Rhiannon, who never take their eyes off me. I am tired and in considerable discomfort, but am overjoyed to see them. Only a day later I am in a two-bed room on the liver ward and learning to walk with a Zimmer frame. That first night on the ward, I sleep a full eight hours, wake the next morning with a sense of levity and grace, and walk to the bathroom without assistance. A week to the day after surgery, I leave the hospital. The consultant who signs me out tells me this equals the record for turnaround on a liver transplant. I am irrepressible and quite barking: mad as a hatter, says the ward sister, Julie, approvingly. On leaving, I thank all the staff who have tended me. I vow to myself that I will never again complain about the National Health Service. As a parting gift they give me a blue plastic container for all my pills, with sections designating the days of the week. I take my pills four times a day. I swallow them down with water, tea or apple juice. They make me whole again. No, that's a lie; they suppress my immune system in order to prevent me from rejecting the new liver. Before long I will have forgotten life without pills, but that is a small price to pay.

I spend the first few days at my sister's house near Skenfrith. I have a strong desire to be in the countryside, to be surrounded by green things. Hilary was a nursing sister in an earlier life and the hospital authorities are keen that I am kept under some kind of medical supervision after being released so promptly: her house is also closer to Birmingham than our home in Cardiff, in case of emergency. I stay there with Rose and the girls and I learn to walk longer distances, even venturing outside and hobbling to the edge of the woods. It is springtime and bluebells carpet the ground. I enjoy this display of nature's renewal with the rapture of a pagan.

While it takes time to get over the physical effects of large-scale surgery — and these are fairly easy to monitor and evaluate — it is much harder to account for the affective responses of the mind to such an experience. After returning to Cardiff, I alternate between a state of mild euphoria and growing uncertainty. The euphoria relates to my survival – the graft has taken well – and the knowledge that my body will recover to full strength and I will soon be able to carry out a fairly normal life. The uncertainty is due to the fact that I am still carrying the hepatitis C virus and it will only be a matter of time before the effects of that begin to materialise in new symptoms. However, I keep this doubt at bay, confident that with my new liver I will be strong enough to withstand the most debilitating effects of the virus for a considerable period of time. I *choose* to believe this, because, frankly, I am emotionally unable to process the relief at my miraculous recovery alongside the possibility of having to combat the effects of the hepatitis all over again. But a month after the operation I suffer a perceptible dip into a melancholic, despondent or depressed state, which I believe to be caused jointly by the effects of medication and financial worries brought on by my decision, the year before, to retire from my lecturing job. I am not expecting this reaction, since, throughout my illness, I have maintained an upbeat and accepting attitude. This trough in my emotional state is deepened by an almost total apathy towards writing, which for many years has been a daily practice, and by which I had intended to make a living following my retirement. Infuriatingly, my writer friends tell me (as I know myself) that the only way to drag myself out of this predicament is by writing.

Over the summer my melancholy becomes routine, and although I am assured that some degree of depression is a common enough consequence of major surgery, and certainly not unusual in the case of transplant recipients, this knowledge does nothing to help. I spend six weeks in the house at Rabós over August and September, but manage to write only three short paragraphs. I have nothing to say, for the moment, and while I am not by any means consistently miserable, it is as if there were a terrible void in the fabric or substance of the world, and that no matter how I might try, there is, in the end, nothing of any value that can fill it. It transpires, on our return to Wales, that I am suffering from haemolytic anaemia, and this would account for my fatigue, listlessness and gloom (if not perhaps for the exaggerated nature of those woeful imprecations against the universe that my family have endured throughout the summer). My haemoglobin levels are dangerously low. I am given several blood transfusions and put on a moderate dose of steroids.

Instead of recovering, I develop the notion, or rather, the conviction, that at the time of my operation, when for a while I had no liver – between the old and the new, as it were – my body thought that it was dead, and resigned itself to perpetual oblivion. I am swayed by the idea that the liver is the controlling organ of the body as well as, according to certain ancient and esoteric traditions, the seat of the soul. This would mean that I have turned into some kind of zombie. Left to nature, I argue, my body would have died in the course of the past few months. My soul knew this, and has pre-emptively fled the body, leaving me no more than a vacant husk. Moreover, I sense an odd ambiguity in the attitude of others towards my miraculous recovery. As Thomas Bernhard wrote in *Wittgenstein's Nephew*, his own demented account of illness experience: "When a sick person, having ceded the place he has once occupied by right, suddenly demands its restitution, the healthy regard this as an act of monstrous presumption. A sick person who returns home always feels like an intruder in an area where he no longer has any business to be."

More weeks pass in a state of mental and emotional inertia. I sleep for ridiculously long spells, as if my body were trying to make up for the years of deprivation. I feel as though I have become 'leftovers' – an expression with which I become fixated, as if my survival were an aberration, which can in no way be justified. Mulling over this new definition of a posthumous existence, I am dismayed, while walking though the neighbourhood one morning, to see a huge billboard with the word LEFTOVERS advertising a brand of butter, a sight which seems to confirm that the phenomenal world is in agreement with my self-diagnosis. I sink to new, unplumbed levels of despondency. I speak with my GP, with whom I have a good relationship. He decides (quite rationally, given my history) that I do not want to go onto medication for depression. I tell him I endure a bizarre form of guilt for not being more grateful, more appreciative of my recovery. On his suggestion, I visit a psychotherapist. Like the GP, she tells me that feelings of desolation and despair are only to be expected when an intense struggle for survival culminates in life-saving surgery.

One night I dream of a silver fox. I have let him out of his cage. He glances at me, as though checking something, then turns and runs before I have time to register that he was not seeking my approval, but escaping before I have time to change my mind and imprison him again. I have no idea where the silver fox goes, or what he does in his secret places, but I do know that he escapes scrutiny by his tireless flight, that he swerves and shimmies through an onslaught of arrows and of huntsmen with their baying hounds. I half awaken, with words running through my mind: *may the god of free things grant him speed and cunning.* I wake properly and say out loud – though there is no one else in the room – *we have entered thick weather.*

In the autumn, I am invited by a Belgian writers' organisation to do a month as writer in residence at a country villa in Flanders. I think that this might be a good idea, but my hepatologist advises against leaving the country for such a long spell. I do, however, go to Brussels on a two-night trip, to take part in a translation workshop and poetry reading. To set me up, the hepatologist prescribes a sharp boost in my prescription of steroids. For the first time in months, I feel fully alive, stay up for two nights with friends in Brussels, and by the time I return home I know I am going to have to make a sustained effort to pull myself out of this hole. Over the winter I begin by putting into some kind of order the haphazard and fragmentary notes that I typed out in the weeks before the operation, and have scribbled in my journal during the delirium of my encephalopathy. Writing helps me gain focus. The story I want to write begins to fall into shape.

39

Montaigne made the sensible declaration towards the end of his life that "every day I dispossess myself of what I have" – which suggests a letting go of artefacts (material and otherwise) which accumulate in the course of a lifetime. Many of us feel we can afford to do this earlier rather than later.

A few years ago, the artist Michael Landy put his every possession on a conveyor belt to be destroyed, everything was crushed, so that he could be cleansed, purged of every last article of *stuff*. I recognise the gesture, acknowledge it, and yet know that it is precisely that, a gesture; there is no leaving the past behind, and these appurtenances of belonging, all the things that require and demand ownership, are merely the outward form of a nostalgia too immense to contain. And although the act of destruction might be viewed superficially as a rejection of consumerism, it is also, more poignantly, an attempt to be rid of one's memories, and of oneself.

Because of this impossible nostalgia (both for the people we once were and for the people we never became, as well as for the people we have lost) we feel the need, from time to time, to begin again, to be free of all the accumulated possessions – or narratives – of a lifetime, to drop everything and set out on a new road. But it is also the case that however many times we do this, in vain pursuit of a simpler, truer version of ourselves, the more baggage we acquire. The discarded versions have left a shadow on the soul, a barely perceptible mark, like a passage of writing that has been deleted, but whose invisible presence continues to haunt the text, leaving the reader with an impression that what he or she has read contains a more substantial quality or truth than the words on their own suggest. It is the silence that lingers in the spaces between the remaining words that make the deepest impression, those resonances of the absent and the lost.

40

April 2008

I am staying in the house at Rabós, one year after the crisis with encephalopathy at the start of this account, one year since I visited the Dance of Death at Verges before returning home for my transplant. There is just me and Bruno the dog. It is not as cold this time around; either that or I don't feel it like I did last year. But I have a fire going in the kitchen. I like the company of flames and the smell of wood smoke.

Someone is playing music close by, near enough to hear the Spanish words quite clearly. Perhaps the Peruvian labourers working on a neighbour's house have a radio. The singer tells of an island, far away, home to many talking birds, who have penetrated the souls of living men and women, causing them to travel the world with this song in their throats, a clutch of bird-people, how they soar, even the countless millions of dead can be heard to stir; even the animal-god who stalks the thorny floor of the dry river gorge that runs down to the sea. Quite a song.

I have started reading *2666*, the posthumously published novel by Roberto Bolaño, which I picked up from the bookshop in Figueres. The prose is brisk and horribly funny, and today I have been thinking, with great sadness, about the book's author, whom I met all those years ago, while working the grape harvest near Lézignan-Corbières. I reflect with sorrow on Roberto's death at fifty, while awaiting his transplant, and me going on, making it to fifty-one, against the odds. These frailties of chance are unspeakable, they render nothing out of nothing, devastate with their random pickings; who shall gain, who shall lose, it all seems so monstrous.

It is a morning of bright sunshine and complex, contrapuntal birdsong. Everything is crystalline after yesterday's rain, and the air smells different, hinting at summer. I throw another log on the fire, breakfast on orange juice, toast and coffee, feed Bruno the dog, and spend another hour reading. Afterwards, I walk along a lane into the woods that extend most of the way towards the coast, a few kilometres to the east of here. If I were to continue along this trail, into the peninsula, I would eventually arrive at Cap Norfeu, the cape of Orpheus, supposedly named after the poet who could sing so sweetly that wild beasts would follow him about and the gods of Hades could be persuaded to give up their dead. It pleases me to think of the eternal poet strumming on his lyre in some cave hidden among the rocks, the waves pounding the shoreline below, the Orpheus of a parallel life, the one that evades the Maenads – wine-crazed women followers of Dionysus – who according to myth tore him limb from limb in their frenzy.

The tracks through the foothills are studded with pine trees, cork and holm oak. Behind, and swathed in blue air, mountains fold into one another like sleeping dragons. At this time of year it is possible to walk for a whole day without seeing a single person. The southern flanks of the Alberas used to be planted with olive, but thousands of trees were destroyed by frost during a particularly cold winter half a century ago and there was neither the workforce nor the population to justify re-planting. The land is no longer farmed, away from the villages. It is now a national park, up to the border with France to the north, and some of the upper reaches serve as pasture for the big Pyrenean cattle. The hillsides are dotted with spring flowers, in violet, blue, white and yellow, plants I recognise but cannot name. Occasionally I pass wild boar tracks, but am unlikely to see any boar at this time of day; they tend to venture out at dusk. However, I do see golden tortoises emerging in the early spring sunshine, and have twice spotted a red fox.

I carry a small rucksack and collect pinecones for the fire in my kitchen. They provide excellent kindling. Bruno approves of pinecones also. Sometimes, if he is lucky, the pinecone serves as a ball; I chuck it and he chases. With cones we both win. So he brings me a collection of them as we amble along the forest path, depositing them at my feet, one at a time, and then lopes off, tail thrashing, leaping at yellow butterflies. I pick up the cones, stash them in my bag, and Bruno, ever alert to the prospect of retrieving things, stops in his tracks to watch me, gives up on the weaving butterflies and bounds off in search of more cones.

While on my walk I begin to think about illness, and of what Susan Sontag had to say about illness being a place with its own rules and customs. I have spent a long while inhabiting the kingdom of the sick, and now it is time to step back into the kingdom of the well. It is as if I hold two passports from countries that are mutually suspicious of each other, the realm of the sick resembling a nervous, oppressed minority, always sensitive to the slights and oversights afforded them by the healthy, while those who occupy the kingdom of the well are, to a large extent, oblivious to the realm of the ill and its denizens living their lives alongside, or in parallel with their own. Those of us who have recently stayed in the kingdom of the ill and are making a tentative return to the land of the healthy are always aware, however, that the slightest trick of fortune will send us careening back towards the other place.

FURTHER READING

References to and quotations from the following publications are gratefully acknowledged, and are listed in the order in which they appear in the book:

Arthur Rimbaud, letter to George Izambard, trans. Wyatt Mason, in *Rimbaud Complete* (Scribner, 2003); Bob Dylan, 'Stuck Inside of Mobile with the Memphis Blues Again', in *Lyrics 1962–2001* (Simon & Schuster, 2004); Italo Calvino, *If on a Winter's Night a Traveller*, trans. William Weaver (Minerva, 1992); Arthur Frank, *The Wounded Healer* (University of Chicago Press, 1997); Susan Sontag, *Illness as Metaphor/AIDS and its Metaphors* (Penguin, 1990); Marguerite Duras, *Practicalities*, trans. Barbara Bray (Flamingo, 1991); Christoph Meckel, 'The Lion', trans. Christopher Middleton, in *German Writing Today* (Penguin, 1967); Michel de Montaigne, 'Travel Journal', trans Donald M Frame in *The Complete Works* (Everyman, 2003); Arthur Rimbaud, 'Roman', in *Rimbaud Complete* (Scribner, 2003); Anthony Beevor, *Crete: The Battle and the Resistance* (Penguin, 1991); Archie Cochrane *One Man's Medicine* (Wiley Blackwell, 1989); Alexander Waugh, *Fathers and Sons* (Headline, 2005); Enrique Vila-Matas, *Bartleby,* trans. Jonathan Dunne (Vintage, 2005); Robert Walser, *The Walk*, trans Christopher Middleton (Serpent's Tail, 1992); Thomas Kinsella (trans.) *The Tain* (OUP, 1970); Vladimir Nabokov, *Speak, Memory* (Penguin, 2000); Jean Giono, *Les Grands Chemins* (Gallimard, 1951); Maurice Blanchot, *The Work of Fire,* trans. Charlotte Mandell (Stanford, 1995); Enrique Vila-Matas, *Montano,* trans. Jonathan Dunne (Vintage, 2007); Don DeLillo, *The Names* (Picador, 1987); Lawrence Durrell, *Prospero's Cell* (Faber & Faber, 1974); Maurice Blanchot, *The Space of Literature*, trans. Ann Smock (University of Nebraska, 1982); Walter Benjamin, *Illuminations*, trans. Harry Zohn (Pimlico, 1999); Yannis Ritsos, 'The Moonlight Sonata', trans. Peter Green and Beverly Bardsley in *The Fourth Dimension* (Anvil, 1993); Roberto Bolaño, *Last Evenings on Earth,* trans. Chris Andrews (Picador, 2008); Joan Didion, 'On keeping a notebook', in *We tell ourselves stories in order to live* (Everyman,

2006); Javier Marías, *Dark Back of Time*, trans. Esther Allen (Chatto & Windus, 2003); Margaret Anne Doody, *The True Story of the Novel* (HarperCollins, 1997); Georges Bataille, *The Cradle of Humanity,* trans. Michelle Kendall and Stuart Kendall (Zone Books, 2009); Holly Howitt, *Desk,* unpublished manuscript; Jorge Luís Borges, 'The South', in *Fictions,* trans. Anthony Kerrigan (Calder, 1991); Roberto Bolaño, 'Literatura + enfermedad = enfermedad' (my translation) in *El gaucho insufrible* (Anagrama, 2003); Andrés Neuman, in *Tres Reaparaciones de Bolaño*, personal correspondence (my translation); Charles Baudelaire, 'Voyaging', in *The Flowers of Evil*, trans. James McGowan (OUP, 1993); Thomas Bernhard, *Wittgenstein's Nephew*, trans. David McLintock (Vintage, 1988); Roberto Bolaño, *2666* (Anagrama, 2004). Nicola Rayner's own account of the events described in Section 36, 'I was abducted at gunpoint', can be found online at www.guardian.co.uk/travel/2006/Oct/17/travelnews.

Acknowledgements

I would like to acknowledge with particular gratitude the doctors, nurses and auxiliary staff at Birmingham's Queen Elizabeth Hospital. Most particularly my thanks are due to Professor Elwyn Elias and Professor Stephen Wigmore, Doctor David Mutimer and Doctor Geoffrey Haydon. I would also like to thank Doctor Andrew Godkin of the University Hospital, Cardiff. My GP, Stephen Glascoe, has been an invaluable ally against the onslaughts of my serial ailments. I would like to thank him also for checking this manuscript for medical veracity.

My heartfelt thanks are also offered to my sister Hilary for the generous use of her home after the operation, my brother David and his wife Siân for their kindness and support, and my father, Cen, for remaining a source of sound wisdom and for attempting to instil in me a consistent moral compass.

My neighbours in Catalunya supplied unfailing friendship, hospitality and good food throughout my illness: Juliette Murphy and Joan Castelló, Ramona Estarriol and my dear friend Lluís Peñaranda who passed away while this book was in preparation. Thanks too to those friends who read the story in draft form: Tessa Hadley, Des Barry, John Williams, David Greenslade, and Rose Gwyn Pallot, *compañera de mi vida*.

Finally, as before, I owe a debt of gratitude to my editor, Gwen Davies, for her astute critical reading, and her unfailing ability to spot the elephant in the bathtub.

Sections of *The Vagabond's Breakfast* have appeared in *New Welsh Review* and *The Reader*. The writing of this book was enabled by a Creative Wales Award from the Arts Council of Wales in 2008. I gratefully acknowledge ACW for its support.

www.alcemi.eu

Talybont Ceredigion Cymru SY24 5HE
e-mail gwen@ylolfa.com
phone (01970) 832 304
fax 832 782

ALCEMI A